Culture, Friendship, and Marriage: Theory and Practice

REV. TOCHI IWUJI

Culture, Friendship, and Marriage:
Theory and Practice
Copyright @ 2024 Marriage and Family Care
Institute

FIRST EDITION

All rights reserved, including the rights to reproduce this book or portions thereof in any form whatever. *No part of this publication may be reproduced, stored in a retrieval system, or transmitted, in any form, by any means, electronic, mechanical, photocopying, recording, or otherwise without the prior permission of the publisher or a license permitting restricted copying.*

Printed in the United States of America

ISBN: 979-8-9909099-1-5

www.FatherTochi.org

Foreword

Beginning with marriage as envisioned in the canon law, moving through considerations of marriage as characterized by friendship and love, indicating the significance of marriage in the context of the Church, and ending with a proposal on mentoring couples before their marriage. This book offers a comprehensive view of the theology of Christian marriage and of how best to catechize engaged couples. It can serve as a valuable resource for pastoral ministers engaged in marriage preparation.

Msgr. David I. Fulton

Table of Contents

Introduction — 9

Chapter 1: The Catholic Church and Marriage — 13

- Properties of Catholic Marriage
- Marriage as a Covenant:
- Marriage as a Vocation
- Marriage as a Sacrament

Chapter 2: Socio-Cultural Reflection on Marriage — 29

- Cultural and Religious Diversity and its Impact on Marriage
- Enculturation
- Inculturation
- Marriage and Inculturation
- Individualism as a Challenge

Chapter 3: The Overlooked Piece in Marriage Preparation and Discussion — 47

- Ancient Idea of Friendship

- Plato
- Aristotle
- Cicero
- Augustine on Friendship
- Aquinas on Friendship
- Incarnation As an Expression of Friendship

Chapter 4: Friendship and Marriage 65

Chapter 5: The Pastoral Application in the Marriage Preparation Process 71

- Marriage as Part of Human Society
- Marriage as Part of Ecclesial Society
- Marriage as a Liturgical Event
- Marriage and its Theological Implications

Chapter 6: Catechumenate as a Model 87

- Marriage Catechumenate
- Marriage Preparation and Tools

Chapter 7: Marriage Mentor Program Proposal 101

- Mentor Couples Characteristics to Consider

- Formation of Mentor Couples
- Mentor Couples Discernment Phase
- Formation of Mentor Couples
- Ministry Structure
- Proposed responses to couples according to the level of engagement

Conclusion	107
Footnotes	109
Resources	121
Author Bio	127
Notes	128

Introduction

Marriage is a natural institution and society with its unique components distinct from any other form of institution. Marriage is in the natural order and *"the intimate partnership of married life and love has been established by the creator and qualified by His laws. It is rooted in the conjugal covenant of irrevocable personal consent. Hence, by human act whereby spouses mutually bestow and accept each other, a relationship arises which by divine will and in the eyes of society too is a lasting one"*.[1] For a long time, Christian theology of marriage was juridically formulated as a contract, the Second Vatican Council brought into focus the covenant nature of marriage. Though marriage is beautiful, the challenges that accompany it make it hard for people to appreciate it or even believe in its sacredness.

Culture and marriage are two concepts that are deeply intertwined in human societies. Culture shapes the norms, values, expectations, and practices of marriage, while marriage influences the transmission, adaptation, and evolution of culture. In this book, we explore the fascinating diversity and complexity of culture and marriage across the world, from ancient times to the present day which means that marriage begins as a secular reality. In addressing the relationship between marriage and human existence, this book addresses one overlooked aspect of our human existence: friendship. Friendship is an integral part of any relationship's success; marriage as a partnership between a man and a woman will flourish better when couples understand that friendship provides a platform for marital love to enhance and be enjoyed. The book will consider human friendship in pre-Christian writings, in Augustine, and Aquinas. There will be a consideration of friendship with God that is made possible by the Incarnation. The human friendship of a married couple can serve as a sign and instrument of friendship with God in Christ. Marital love expresses a friendship not limited to an individual couple but is best situated within the body of Christians, particularly within the Christian Church.

How married couples are prepared needs to be evaluated, and attention should be given to how we help them appreciate what they are consenting to. Preparing for marriage requires a cooperative endeavor on the part of the parish minister and the couple preparing for marriage. In this endeavor, it must be noted that there may be blind spots, both on the part of the couple and the minister. New attention is needed to reveal better the essential impact friendship has in marriage. The couple's blind spots may be centered around issues of expressive individualism and a resultant silo-morality, compromised faith, or lack of faith, resulting in ignoring or dismissing the role of the Church in marriage. The parish minister's blind spots may be centered on an excessive preoccupation with the goods of fidelity, permanence, and procreation, excluding the *bonum coniugum* – the good of the spouses that needs to be understood, chosen, and actuated within the marriage covenant. Moreover, the parish minister's focus on the canonical contract of marriage, with its emphasis on freedom to marry and sufficiency of consent, might well wind up ignoring the essentials of marriage as a sacrament and, thus, an act of worship.

The Pontifical Council for the Family has provided insights on the need for reevaluating the marriage preparation process to accommodate the dynamics of marriage currently. The document states,

> *"The importance of this preparation involves a process of evangelization which is both maturation and deepening the faith. If the faith is weak or almost nonexistent, it must be revived. Thorough, patient instruction that arouses and nourishes the ardor of a living faith cannot be excluded. Especially where the environment has become paganized, it will be advisable to offer a journey of faith, similar to the catechumenate, and a presentation of the fundamental Christian truths that may help acquire or strengthen the maturity of the faith of the persons contracting marriage. The favorable moment of marriage preparation should be transformed, as a*

sign of hope, into a New Evangelization for future families." 2

In light of the difficulties surrounding the possible blind spots of both couple and minister, an adequate catechesis on the sacrament of matrimony and a renewed marriage preparation will need to include the following considerations: marriage as part of human society, marriage as part of ecclesial society, marriage as a liturgical event, 'marriage, and its theological implications.' This book is intended for anyone interested in learning more about the rich and diverse aspects of culture and marriage, and the dynamic relationship between them. We hope that this book will inspire readers to reflect on their own cultural and marital experiences and to appreciate the diversity and complexity of human cultures and marriages.

Chapter 1
Catholic Church and Marriage

The Catholic Church has been at the forefront crusade to teach its faithful that marriage is a unique institution with its origin in God. Archbishop Fulton Sheen stated, "The Church sees each aspect of marriage as the reflection, the echo, or the shadow cast by some great divine truth."[2] The Church clearly understands the revelatory reality of marriage that she holistically approaches her teaching. The church sees marriage as a secular reality; she sees it as a covenant and a calling in which a man and a woman come together to witness the firm and unbroken bond between Christ and the church. The church helps her faithful understand the dynamism of God's love expressed in marital love and helps her faithful understand how Christ raised their marriage to the dignity of a sacrament. In this chapter, I shall explore the components of Catholic marriage, marriage as a covenant, marriage as a vocation, and why we believe marriage is a sacrament.

Properties of Catholic Marriage:

The Church's teaching on the essential properties of marriage is drawn from her understanding and teaching on the sacramentality of the institution of marriage. According to Michael G. Lawler, *"the essential properties of marriage, unity, and indissolubility, must be understood in the context of sacramental marriage defined as the intimate community of the whole of life."*[3] This idea of the properties of marriage needs to be understood in its right context, the code of Canon Law number 1056 clearly states what the sacramentality of marriage brings to the already existing union between a man and a woman. The Code states, *"The essential properties of marriage are unity and indissolubility, which in Christian marriage obtain a special firmness because of the sacrament."*[4] This code establishes these properties of unity and indissolubility as essential to any marriage; it goes further to state that in Christian marriage, these properties apply to other forms of marriage, such as civil and traditional marriages. Marriage acquires characteristic stability through its sacramentality.

If the essential properties of marriage are unity and insolubility, why does the church approve some marriages and not others? Christian marriages in the catholic Church acquire specific characteristics that establish marriage as valid or invalid. The church only dissolves the sacramental marriage as invalid because that marriage was never consummated; that is, there was no sexual activity after the sacrament celebration. The church believes in the indissolubility of marriage in fidelity to the words of Jesus but also considers another aspect of the ecclesiastical policy and judgment about the dissolution of marriage. They establish two conditions in which any marriage is indissoluble; those conditions are that the marriage must be sacramental and consummated. There are specific nuances to these conditions, but it is not my intention to delve into those; my intention here is to explore these properties and why a marriage, even though secular reality, acquires such significant value for the Catholic church. The conditions stated above are the results of various historical discourses. Lawler says,

> *"that marriage was created by God. No Catholic theologian would debate it. That the marriage bond becomes indissoluble, even in a sacramental marriage, only when the marriage is consummated is a nuance added by Gratian in the twelfth century to resolve the debate between the Roman and Northern European opinions about what makes a marriage."* [5]

Jesus' injunction, which declares, **"What God has joined together, let no man divide,"** for several years, the church understood and taught it to be a moral demand from the Lord. In the twelfth century, the Gratian brought a new twist to that injunction; it began to be understood as an ontological reality and not just a moral demand. Lawler remarks thus, *"They should not give way to cannot, as in a ratified and consummated marriage cannot be dissolved by any human power or for any reason other than death."* [6]

Mackin references code 1013 in the 1917 code of the Code of Canon Law paragraph two, which states the essential properties of marriage remarks thus,

> *"The canon saves a place for the radical possibility of polygamous marriage and dissolution by adding that monogamy and indissolubility gain a unique firmness in the marriages of Christians because of their sacramental character. In other merely natural marriages, monogamy is exceptionable, and indissolubility is dissoluble."* [7]

Mackin addresses essential components here, the free consent of a man and a woman and their intention to commit themselves to a faithful and perpetual relationship. Nevertheless, the church adding another nuance to the injunction of Christ with her stance on sacramental and consummated marriage being indissoluble presents a question about how the church determines if a sacramental marriage is consummated.

I don't intend to address the responses to this critical question here but to remark that,

> *"Pius XI suggested the answer lies in 'the mystical meaning of Christian marriage,' namely, its reference to that 'most perfect union which exists between Christ and the church.' Though it does not specify as precisely as Pius that the consummated sacramental marriage is indissoluble, the International Theological Commission offers the exact reason for the indissolubility of Christian marriage lies in the fact that it is the sacrament, the image of the indissoluble union between Christ and the Church."* [8]

Marriage as a Covenant:

Covenant is an essential concept in the Scripture. God has always been the initiator of every covenant, as we see in his covenant with Noah, Abraham, Moses, and, more importantly, his covenant with the people of Israel. The belief in the creative power of Yahweh demythologized marriage and spared marriage and sexuality from all mystical confusion; based on the premise, other ideas emerged in their understanding of marriage and human sexuality as Schillebeeckx stated that, *"in addition to this idea of marriage, another grew up in Israel, namely that marriage was the means of revealing the community existing between Yahweh and his people. It can be claimed without reserve that Israel regarded marriage between human beings as a representation of and a reference to the covenant of grace between Yahweh and his people."* [9] Like every saving reality between Yahweh and his people, he always expressed it in human terms, and the critical factor is not the reality expressed in human terms but the saving reality itself. A good grasp of the core reality in understanding Christian marriage as a covenant will help us put in the proper perspective the imperfections experienced in marriage, as there are no reasons to quit marriage or discredit the institution of marriage as something of divine origin. Schillebeeckx puts it thus,

> *"The married life of human beings, with all the ups and downs, its certainties about the past and the uncertainties about the future, with the recollective pleasures of happiness enjoyed and the more bitter memories of hard times, infidelity, and the deprivation of love, all these formed the prism through which the prophets saw the saving covenant of his people and enabled the people to comprehend the covenant. Human marriage became the means of revealing the covenant of salvation."* [10]

The prophets tried to express in concrete terms the reality of God's saving covenant with a natural institution we can easily relate to and understand. We see that this was played out by Hosea in appealing to a secular reality to buttress the community of grace between Yahweh and the people of Israel. *"Hosea effected a demythologizing of the marriage image by calling these sexual motives and the religious cult itself 'harlotry' when he took marriage over as an image of relationship within a covenant."* [11]   His marriage to Gomer was a precursor for God's saving actions among his people. Marriage as a covenant, therefore, is approached from the perspective of the unconditional love of Yahweh for his people. The couple commits to each other in mutual fidelity, which involves an intimate knowledge of selves in a manner that is not broken or abused.

The image of marriage as a revelatory reality of the covenant between God and his people also reoccurs in the New Testament. The New Testament reveals Jesus as the fulfillment of that covenant, which establishes a new covenant that cannot be broken by anything. According to Schillebeeckx, "the covenant relationship between Christ and his church is a marriage relationship, and it was represented by Paul according to the various phases of marriage, loving surrender, cleansing, the marriage ceremony, and the union and loving care of married love."[12] The creative episode which situates God's intent for his creation and also establishes a loving relationship between a man and a woman acquires an in-depth insight into the New Testament. Schillebeeckx remarks

> *"If we can justify man's creation theologically in grace, we should be able to understand better now than we were able to know from the Old Testament that the concrete gift of creation, which is marriage, could become the appointed means of revealing and expressing, in a human and religious manner, God's covenant of grace with men in Christ, and that this use of the image could illuminate some of the deepest aspects of marriage itself."* [13]

Without understanding marriage as a covenant, other aspects of marriage, like its properties, will not be something to be valued or upheld. In this understanding, marriage becomes a sign of humanity and a channel of the grace of the couple and their family. The writer of Proverbs in chapter 2:17-17 indicates that marriage is a sacred covenant when it says, **"wisdom will save you also from the adulterous woman, from the wayward woman with her seductive words, who has left the partner of her youth and ignored the covenant she made before God."** [14] The theme of marriage as a covenant has been one that is unique in the catholic understanding of marriage. The Catholic Church understands marriage to be a Covenant between a man and a woman which expresses in a concrete human way the covenantal love between God and his people, a sign of the covenant between Christ and the church.

Marriage as a Vocation

Vocation is a calling in which someone higher than us invites us to journey with him on a specific path and for a specific purpose. Marriage is not like any form of social institution, but a supernatural calling and sacrament given by Christ. *"As with every vocation, marriage must be understood within the primary vocation to love, because humanity 'is created in the image and likeness of God whom himself love. In baptism, God is faithful to grow in love and a vocation to grow in holiness, for greater participation in God's holiness."* [15] Every human person must discover their vocation and be willing to follow that vocation with clear intention and will. There are many vocations, and marriage is one of those vocations with which God blessed humanity. According to Francis Nemeck and Marie Coombs, "the vocation to marriage in effect comprises two callings: one, to matrimony in general as a basic lifestyle; the other, to marriage with a specific person as one's life partner. Thus, God invites a man and a woman to commit themselves in love to each other and God in the context of a conjugal way of life until the death of one of them."[16] Marriage must be affirmed by all as a real divine calling like any other vocation, such as the Religious Life and Priesthood. In marriage, God invites men and women to a mission that he entrusts to them with its accompanying graces. Javier Abad and Eugenio Fenoy remark, *"Every vocation is a calling to accomplish some specific mission. It demands a concrete response, a willingness to be God's instrument to carry out freely and responsibility the task one has been entrusted with."* [17] This mission of married life comes with God, which establishes the man and the woman being joined together to accomplish the mission he entrusts them with. Like any other vocation in marriage,

> *"the vocation to married life encompasses a threefold consecration. God makes a husband and wife holy in three interrelated ways. 1. by the grace celebrated in baptism and confirmation, God has already celebrated each of them to God. In matrimony, the Lord deepens that consecration by enabling both spouses to intensify their relationship with the Trinity. 2. In matrimony, the spouses also consecrate themselves to each other. They declare before God and society that they need to let God sanctify the one through the other: the husband through the wife and the wife through the husband. 3. In marriage, God consecrates them as a couple as 'one' to God."* [18]

This mission entrusted to the spouse by God comes with its evangelical dimension because it is not just about their holiness and sanctification, but it is a mission that impacts all humanity by their witness of God's unconditional love expressed in their covenant married relationship. In this awareness of the call to holiness for themselves and their witness to that to the world, their vocation is made apparent. The United States Catholic Bishops remark,

> *"The marital vocation is not a private or merely personal affair. Yes, marriage is a profoundly personal union and relationship, but it is also for the good of the Church and the entire community. The Second Vatican Council teaches that 'the well-being of the person and both human and Christian society is closely bound up with the healthy state of marriage and the family'. As a vocation, or call from God, marriage has a public and ecclesial status within the Church. Catholic spouses ordinarily exchange marital consent within a church setting, before a priest or deacon. The living out of marriage occurs within the whole Body of Christ, which serves and finds nourishment."* [19]

The couple receives this mission and apostolate to the world as fruits of their life of service to God and neighbors as Regis and Libbie Flaherty quoting *Lumen Gentium,* clearly note,

> *"Married couples and Christian parents should follow their proper path (to holiness) through faithful love. They should sustain one another in grace throughout the entire length of their lives. They should embue their offspring, and lovingly welcome them as God's gift, with Christian doctrine and evangelical virtues. In this manner, they offer all men the example of unwearyingly and generous love; in this way, they build up the brotherhood of charity; in so doing, they stand as the witnesses and cooperators in the fruitfulness of the Holy Mother Church; by such lives, they are a sign and participation in that same love, with which Christ loved His Bride and for which He delivered Himself up for her."* [20]

Marriage, understood in this way equips the couples to truly witness to the world firmly and faithfully which expresses God's unfailing love for the world. Marriage, understood as a vocation, helps us to know that real vocation does not in any way separate the nature and identity of the human person from the mission they are entrusted with. Daniel Zopoula remarks, *"When a person chooses marriage, they also choose a tool that God can use to form them and them in the image of God, to encourage and refresh the church, the bride of Christ."* [21]

God provides the enabling grace to accompany the couple in living out their calling in an authentic way, and we respond in gratitude with an awareness that we are here on earth to fulfill God's creative plan for his creation. Marriage is a stable institution in which God clearly expresses his creative intent for a man and a woman. According to Frantz Mars, *"Marriage is a true vocation, a stable and permanent way of life with its basic structure determined by God who instituted marriage."* [22]

Marriage as a Sacrament

Marriage was never considered a sacrament until 1563 when the Council of Trent declared that marriage properly was one of the seven sacraments. The idea that marriage was sacred, and a vocation has always been there in history, people believe too, that marriage was a way of participating in the life of the church and hence, a witness. What the church struggled to establish was that marriage was one of the seven sacraments and this took a series of developments. The Council of Trent established marriage as one of the seven sacraments and pronounced an *anathema* on anyone who taught or believed otherwise. Philip Reynolds referencing the Council's decision remarks, *"These sacraments are collectively necessary for salvation, for 'faith in the divine promise' does not suffice. Each sacrament contains a grace that it signifies, conferring it ex opera operato on any recipient who puts no obstacle in its way."* [23] The discourse on marriage as a sacrament as established by the Council of Trent was derived from how the sacrament plays a role in the history and economy of salvation. Marriage is not just a sacrament in terms of how the creation episode confirms the indissolubility of marriage; it is also a sacrament in the New Covenant established by Christ himself.

Marc Cardinal Ouellet quoting *Gaudium et Spes* remarks,

> *"Authentic married love is caught up in divine love. It is governed and enriched by Christ's redeeming power and the saving activity of the Church so that this love may lead the spouses to God with powerful effect and may aid and strengthen them in the sublime office of being a father or a mother. For this reason, Christian spouses have a special sacrament by which they are fortified and receive a kind of consecration in the duties and dignity of their state."* [24]

In marriage, the couple takes up this indissoluble bond which expresses the unfailing love of Christ for the church, and they receive a special grace to enable them to carry out their duties in dignity and love. Marriage, lived as a sacramental bond, becomes an avenue through which the couple uniquely encounters the grace of God. *"Christian marriage becomes an efficacious sign, the sacrament of the covenant of Christ and the Church. An efficacious sign does not merely symbolize or signify something but makes present what it signifies."* [25] Marriage truly signifies to baptized couples the love Christ has for the Church and makes it a reality. By presenting marriage as a sacrament, the scripture uses a human reality already known in society to make the relationship between Christ and the Church obvious. This shows that Christ's love for the Church surpasses the natural love of the human person, so *"Christian marriage aspires not only to natural human love but to Christ's love for the Church."* [26] Married men and women are invited to imitate Christ, and only in the sacrament of matrimony can this imitation be possible and an opportunity to share in Christ's love. Marriage makes it possible for the couple to present Christ's self-gift of love through their mutual self-gift of self in fidelity which endures to the end.

Marriage becomes a sacrament when the couple brings their marital relationship to its fullness through conjugal love in fidelity to each other, making it indissoluble. Michael G. Lawler puts it thus, *"a sacramental marriage becomes indissoluble only when marital love on which it is founded attains its practical faithful as a communion that is mutually faithful and loyal, that is mutually giving way, and that is mutually servant. Even sacramental marriage acquires indissolubility only when, and because, the marital love that grounds it has become faithful and indissoluble."* [27] Through the mutual exchange of consent, the Holy Spirit binds them together in a covenant of love that is not broken until death. *"the same love that defines the Church now defines the communion between the two spouses: 'authentic married love is caught up into divine love and is directed and enriched by the redemptive power of Christ and the salvific action of the church."* [28] The married couple receives the grace of the sacrament because *"Christ dwells with them, gives them strength to take up their crosses and so follow him, to rise again after they have fallen, to forgive one another, to bear one another's burdens, to 'be subject to one another out of reverence for Christ,' and to love one another with supernatural, tender and fruitful love."* [29] The married couple receives special enablement through the sacrament to fulfill their duties of love for each other and carry these acts authentically and firmly.

Chapter 2
Socio-Cultural Reflection on Marriage:

Man is a cultural animal, and our activities are influenced by the collective and individual appropriation of our cultural principles and values. The United States is a culture of its own; in it exists other cultural connections that become a culture in a culture.

The United States is one of the world's most diverse nations; its strength lies in that diversity, yet its diversity comes with various forms of challenges and tensions. Diversity is never a negative phenomenon but can be very overwhelming, and all of us can witness the effects on society as well as the church, especially as it concerns various values, such as marriage and human relationships. In this chapter, I will explore how these diversities pose a significant challenge to the sacramentality of marriage and the forms these effects are felt. This chapter addresses how diversity impacts marriage, enculturation, inculturation, and the relationship between inculturation and marriage as a tool in such a diverse nation like the United States.

Cultural and Religious Diversity and its Impact on Marriage

The American worldview is, in a way, guided by two cultural influences: religion and law. It is in these two significant cultural influences that marriage is understood and practiced. The *National Directory for Catechesis* remarks, "The United States enjoys a rich community life that an emphasis on pluralism and individual freedom has sustained."[30] The diversity we experience religiously and culturally today differs from that experienced in the past when we had mostly homogenous immigrant communities staying together and supporting each other within a community. Today, many people who identify as a specific ethnicity do so with little or no cultural consciousness. This diversity impacts how marriage is understood and how married relationship is lived.

In the past, couples saw the success of their marriage depended on the community and society's support when people indeed saw their role as witnesses and support for the success of the couples. Currently, couples tend to look within themselves for the success of their union, and people in their lives become spectators instead of witnesses. Another reason that contributes to the diversity is that people move around for economic reasons, and they lose something of themselves and their culture and religion. In contrast, in the past, people lived, married, and raised their children within a community. Andrew Cherlin also remarks that "moving is also a way for young adults to avoid parental supervision. All this may make Americans appear restless. And all these can affect family stability."[31] These realities show how cultural and religious diversity in the United States impacts marriage as an institution and how people respond to the Church's teaching on marriage as a permanent union. Each culture is different, and the difference in cultures influences their understanding of relationships.

Edward P. Wimberly speaking about the struggle of role-playing in relationships and marriage among the African American population remarks that "while it appears to me that there are deeper marital and family dynamics at work in this marriage and families than the religious values that are articulated, the fact is that some marriages and families organize their conflict around religious values."[32] The same is true for other cultures; some cultures have religion embedded in their cultural ideals, while some of their culture and religion are independent. It is easier for some to bring their individual preferences or standards under the scrutiny of religion, while for others, it is hard. These realities impact marriage today and have increased the divorce rate and cohabitation, which opposes God's plan for marriage. The consequence of the diversity of culture and religion in America is what Cherlin argues "American religion, in its focus on both marriage and self-development, tends to encourage marriage, promote an individualistic mode of thinking about personal life, tolerate divorce, and accept or even encourage remarriage. It also encourages cohabiting couples to end their relationship within a few years if they are unwilling to marry."[33] The teaching on Sacramental marriage stands in opposition to such an atmosphere that claims to be religious yet interprets spiritual mysteries such as marriage on their terms. Cultural and Religious diversity confronts the Church with the need to refine the meaning of marriage or, worse, allow society to define marriage for everyone. Cohabitation and divorce are symptoms of the crisis caused by the tension caused by these diversities that challenge who we are as religious and social beings. In some cases, as *Amoris Laetitia* remarks, "the choice of a civil marriage or, in many cases, of simple cohabitation, is often not motivated by prejudice or resistance to a sacramental union, but by cultural or contingent situations."[34] People still hold sacramental marriage as ideal, but because of some situations that confront them and not knowing what to do, they settle for civil marriage or one form of partnership.

Enculturation

Culture is a dynamic phenomenon that takes different forms and aspects. we speak of enculturation, acculturation, and inculturation as other aspects, but for the aim of the thesis, I shall discuss two of these aspects of culture; enculturation and inculturation.

Enculturation is a process in which the human person inserts themself into a culture as a cultural person. The process of inserting into a culture entails socialization and acquiring the knowledge of the 'dos' and 'don'ts' of the culture he finds. Enculturation differs from acculturation, which is a person's encounter with a culture other than theirs and response to the changes therein. Enculturation makes it possible for the individual to learn the order of society and how to conform to it.

The result of enculturation is to establish the human person's identity within a society as a responsible member of that society. According to Stephen Grunian and Marvin Mayers, "Enculturation is the process by which individuals acquire the knowledge, skills, attitudes, and values that enable them to become functioning members of their societies."[35] Enculturation impacts the individual as an integral person, affecting both the conscious and unconscious of the person, making it possible for the individual to achieve proficiency in their culture and internalize the culture in a meaningful manner. Grunian and Mayers argue that,

> *Enculturation begins before birth and continues until death. Thus, children learn respect for the nation's symbols through reciting the Pledge of Allegiance and singing the national anthem. They learn behavior appropriate to their sex, social class, and peer group. They become aware of their reciprocal rights and privileges as well as responsibilities vis-à-vis other persons (e.g., parents, teachers, friends, store clerks, strangers).*[36]

In establishing the individual's identity within the society, the society seeks to make its members responsible and expects that from its members. The process of being enculturated within a society takes two forms: formal and informal, through education and everyday parenting, and nurturing. Enculturation helps determine how a person thinks, behaves, and believes because of how they can interpret experiences based on the culture they find themself. A person's interpretation of an event or experience usually depends on their culture. LeNora Millen speaks of enculturation. Thus,

> *the roles of the adults in my culture, i.e., home, school, and church, were forms of enculturation, which impacted my thinking and my ability to interact with people of*

different backgrounds, genders, and classes. When looking into the effects of assimilation or enculturation within my culture, members of the minority group appeared to emulate the dominant group's culture. These individuals appeared to acquire and hold onto some rank or position within the group. For example, for groups that immigrate to the United States, the process of enculturation to the dominant Anglo-American culture may include, as necessary, learning the English language, changing eating habits, adopting new value systems, and altering the spelling of the family surname. The ability to evolve or transform self within a new culture is difficult for many to fathom, possibly because this process may appear odd and far removed from the innateness of who and what the individual professes or regards as sacred. [37]

Enculturation is, therefore, the first step to inculturation. Mariasusai Dhavamony reechoes some of the ideas represented so far thus,

> *The process of learning one's culture is called enculturation. This is, in essence, a process of conscious or unconscious conditioning exercised within the limits sanctioned by a given body of customs. During childhood, it is essentially a*

> *matter of conditioning to fundamentals-habits of eating, sleeping, speaking, and personal cleaning, which has its significance in shaping the personality and forming the habit patterns of the adult in later life. However, enculturation is an ongoing process through adolescence and adulthood. The specific difference in adult life is that the individual's conscious acceptance or rejection range continuously increases as he grows older. The new forms of behavior presented to him after that are mostly in the realm of culture change or the process of acculturation.[38]*

Though enculturation is often associated with socialization, they are distinct. Both are processes that involve learning and internalizing the norms, values, and behaviors of a society or a culture. Enculturation links the gap between culture and culture as the total behavior of a person, a cultural person. Socialization is the general process of acquiring the skills and knowledge necessary for effective participation in social life. It is a broader concept that includes learning how to interact with others in a way that is appropriate for one's culture. Enculturation is the specific process of learning the culture of one's society. It is a narrower concept that refers to learning the beliefs, values, customs, and symbols of one's culture.

Enculturation is the means through which culture is conserved, it gives culture its stability and "helps to consolidate and continue the existing tradition in times of most rapid change and also a psychological mechanism for the perpetuation of cultural forms."[39] Enculturation then establishes the context in which inculturation finds its relevance and credence as a way of looking out how to make sacramental marriage confront the challenges posed by the diversity of culture in the United States. I will, therefore, briefly explore inculturation.

Inculturation

Inculturation has been used to denote different things by different people and it becomes so confusing what we mean by the term inculturation. It needs to be clearly stated that inculturation is not an adaptation, not implantation, not transplantation, not injection, and not also confrontation. Inculturation is a solid theological discourse, especially in our time, in a manner that corresponds to the consideration of the salvific event in Jesus Christ. George Maduakolam Okorie speaking of inculturation as a method writes that inculturation

> *"may be defined as the process of interpreting and living Christianity (that is, Christian faith and practice) from within the perspective of a particular culture and of its people's social and historical life experience in such a way that Christian values are made to animate the people's way of life. It involves a mutual interaction and influence between culture and the Christian faith whereby the culture is transformed in the process, and Christianity is reinterpreted in the light of a new culture and historical life experience."* [40]

Inculturation takes a series of processes to achieve the purpose for which it is intended; it utilizes the resources available in the culture under discourse, it understands the good news of Jesus as necessary to challenge the culture, and inculturation takes place from the perspective of the culture and within the culture itself. Inculturation takes an interpretative pattern in achieving its aim, and the term appears in a theological sense as used by Joseph Mason in 1962. Okorie writes,

> *"After themes on the agenda of the Second Vatican Council, Mason demanded an inculturated Catholicity, an opening of the Church to the world's cultures. He wrote of inculturation as a*

dynamic process whereby the gospel is proclaimed in a new cultural context, utterly different from the original cultural background of the gospel itself. The ground for this idea was a parallel theological association between 'inculturation' and 'incarnation.' In this way, the process of evangelization in the history of the world was conceptually comparable to how the logos became incarnate, that is to say, to how the Word of God became man in Jewish culture at the time of the Roman Empire." [41]

On another note, Fr. Pedro Arrupe, in 1977 in the Synod on Catechesis, *"maintains that inculturation is a solution to the problem of the real influence of faith on culture, and its absence is one of the main obstacles to evangelization. Catechesis presupposes the inculturation of the faith."* [42] Faith must be communicated to the people in their most profound life experience to the point that it inspires the people's way of life in words and deeds. In this sense, engaged couples are helped to conform to the challenge of the culture they are coming from and integrate into the church's teaching on marriage that is in opposition to societal tendencies and ideologies. Inculturation allows the Word of God to be shared within the rich diversities of human expressions in a relevant and objective manner. Okorie reiterates

Arrupe's definition of inculturation to buttress this point; he writes,

> "Inculturation is the incarnation of Christian faith and the Christian message in a particular cultural context in such a way that this experience not only finds expression through elements proper to the culture in question (this alone would be no more than a superficial adaptation) but becomes a principle that animates, directs and unifies the culture, transforming and remaking it to bring about a new creation." [43]

Incarnation has been an excellent tool to help us appreciate what inculturation means instead of implying our sentiments into the theological concept of inculturation. Okorie provides an elaborate analysis of the relationship between inculturation, and incarnation as expressed in the Apostolic Exhortation *Catechesi Tradendae*; he writes,

> "Catechesis can propose to culture the knowledge of the hidden mystery and help them arise from their living tradition original expressions of the Christian life, celebration, and thought. So, after presenting the various conditions that should mark the relationship between catechesis and culture, he set out to explain that catechesis has an incarnational dimension. 'Genuine catechists know that catechesis 'take flesh' in the

> *various cultures and milieu. Through the mystery of incarnation, the Word of God took human nature. Through the process of inculturation, catechesis, which is a form of proclaiming the gospel, acquires cultural expression."* [44]

The Word of God, therefore, must be the starting point of our inculturation efforts if we must achieve what it ought to achieve. Inculturation understood as incarnational becomes an intimate transformation of the authentic cultural values of a people through the integration of the Word of God and Christian values. Therefore, any inculturation enterprise must always submit to the scrutiny of the Word of God and the Church. The integration of the gospel message in a culture that is so diverse like the United States must be made with discernment, respect, and adherence to the church's guidelines and principles. It should be noted that,

> *"the concept of the inculturation process is a continuous critical interaction between the Christian faith and culture, a developing process, which means that, in the light of the values of the gospel, both the accompanying culture and the culture due to their imperfect nature, are constantly subjected to interrogation order to correct and complete them. Hence, the*

encounter between the Church (the bearer of the Christian faith) with cultures involves the Church's transmission of Christian values to these cultures, at the same time taking the good elements that already exist in them and renewing them from within." [45]

The church must try to understand the wave of cultural diversity and its challenge to the sacraments such as the sacrament of matrimony to properly incarnate the gospel message and catholic teaching in the culture. The culture is always dynamic and not having a proper understanding of that reality puts the church and the culture in an opposing dilemma.

Marriage and Inculturation

Inculturation can become a tool for the church in dealing with the diversity of culture and its challenge to sacramental marriage in our time. I am using inculturation as a tool as it applies the theme under discourse, the challenge of diversity of culture, as it affects the objectivity of sacramental marriage. Marriage is a sacrament's presupposition and must be the foundation for inculturation. As a sacrament lies the belief that marriage is ordained by God and raised to the dignity of a sacrament by Christ; therefore, this belief belongs to the truth of the Scripture. There would not have been any tension if there were no human dimensions to the whole discussion on the objectivity of sacramental marriage.

The challenge of cultural diversity with its accompanying issues stands in opposition to the objectivity of sacramental marriage and the public witness of married love, which involves mutual self-giving in a committed permanent manner that is open to the procreation and education of children. The church must pay attention to the dynamism that accompanies diversity in the United States and understand how to address the crisis of faith and rejection of the catholic faith, especially as it concerns sacramental marriage and what it entails. One of the obstacles to accepting the objectivity of sacramental marriage with its implications on the couple is the issue of individuality and lack of commitment as the culture tends to promote an opposing idea of relationship and life.

Culture is a way of life of a people appropriated by an individual and therefore conditions how each individual responds to things or ideals. Marriage is one of those ideas that is approached or lived based on the cultural realities of a people. Individualism as a cultural ideal in the United States shows how marriage in America differs from marriage in European nations or African nations. Marriage and other forms of relationships, such as cohabitation in the United States, prove to be more delicate than is experienced in other countries. Families in America undergo more transitions than in other nations, and culture plays a key role in the transitions. In addition to moving a lot and the breakdown of ethnic communities, cultural influences such as the media and the internet particularly music, TV shows, movies, and video games promote individualism, promiscuity, and violence. There is tension between marriage as a desired institution to raise a family and individualism as a sought-after means for self-satisfaction. There is a contradictory highlight on marriage as a value desired and individualism as a culture in the United States. According to Andrew Cherlin, "Culture often contains multiple, inconsistent ways of viewing the same reality, and individuals choose, sometimes without even realizing it, which view to adopt."[46] Marriage as an institution is interpreted by different people using different cultural models.

Individualism as a Challenge:

Marriage is generally seen as the noble way to raise a family. Amid the tension between marriage as a desired value and individualism as a cultural ideal, marriage for some is certainly a way to live an adult life; some think it is what everyone does, while for some, you must marry or be in some sort of relationship. The impact of the individualistic cultural ideal on the traditional meaning of marriage today is expressed in what Cherlin calls the American cultural model of marriage. He suggests, "Marriage is the best way to live one's family life, a marriage should be a permanent, loving relationship, a marriage should be a sexually exclusive partnership, and divorce should be a last resort."[47] These elements are still upheld by many, but individualism especially expressive individualism has redefined what marriage implies. Before the nineteenth century, the values of marriage as the desired way to raise a family and divorce as the last resort were not a big problem for most people. The Nineteenth century came with it a new wave in the cultural models, the expressive individualism that flourished as many people sought to explore their sense of self. In the quest to explore, marriage and intimate relationships seek to see "self-development and personal satisfaction as the key rewards of an intimate partnership."[48] Marriage as a covenant between a man and a woman open to procreation and education of children for life is challenged by a cultural model that sees self-development and satisfaction as a reward.

The individualistic cultural ideal become a challenge confronting marriage today; even though marriage is desired and ought to be for life in good times and bad times, people abandon it when in their judgment, it no longer meets their need for self-development. *The Rites* clearly states that "Christian couples, therefore, are to strive to nourish and develop their marriage by undivided affection, which wells up from the fountain of divine love: in a merging of the human and the divine, they remain faithful in body and in, in good times as in bad."[49] Individualism cannot strive to nourish with undivided affection since the key reward in a relationship is self-development and personal satisfaction. It isn't easy to approach marriage with the attitude of giving and accepting love and mutual growth. Divorce and cohabitation become the effects of the enormous impact individualistic cultural ideals have on marriage today. People move in and out of a marriage once they are no longer happy or their personal needs are not met. The individualistic mindset impacts marriage as an institution and questions the components of marriage as an institution. Individualistic cultural ideal questions why marriage must be a partnership of whole life and why one worries about children since an intimate relationship is to serve the "self" and not to care for another human being. The impact extends to why some people qualify some divorce as "good" and some have questioned the Church's stand on some sexual ethical issues like abortion and contraception. The idea of sex is always positive, in counseling couples I have found that it is often one of the primary sources of conflict.

Chapter Three
The overlooked piece in Marriage preparation and discussion Ancient Idea of Friendship

Plato

Although his symposium is devoted to the consideration of love, Plato seems not to have written much on friendship; yet, in *Lysis,* he provides a very valuable foundation for any good discussion on friendship. In *Lysis,* Plato puts these comments in Socrates' mouth:

> "Friendship is the union of two persons in mutual affection and remembrance of one another. The friend can do for his friends what he cannot do for himself. He can give him counsel in times of difficulty; he can teach him 'to see himself as others see him'; he can stand by him when all the world is against him; he can gladden and enlighten him by his presence; he can

> *divide sorrows, he can double his joys; he can anticipate his wants. He will discover ways of helping him without creating a sense of his superiority; he will find out his mental trials, but only that he may minister to them. Among true friends' jealousy has no place: they do not complain of one another for making new friends, or for not revealing some secret of their lives; (in friendship there must be reserves) they do not intrude upon one another, and they mutually rejoice in any good which happens to either of them, though it may be to the loss of the other. They may live apart and have little intercourse, but when they meet, the old tie is as strong as ever according to the common saying, they find one another always the same."* [50]

Plato addresses friendship as directed toward the universal form of love, but which emanates from specific affective attachments. He believes that "friendship moves from mutual attraction to ideal beauty and goodness."[51]

Plato in *Lysis* has explored Socrates' question on what *friend* truly means. He makes an important distinction between friendship and the casual sexual relationship often portrayed today as a "friends-with-benefits" relationship. David Bolotin writes, "Lysis and Menexenus, in addition to being friends, are probably the two youngest interlocutors of Plato's Socrates. Their age helps to explain what might otherwise appear to be a serious omission from the dialogue. For there is no reference in it to the durability which is ordinarily said to distinguish true from causal friendship or merely sexual love."[52] Nevertheless, Plato underscores stability and a pledge of trust as basic to the establishment and sustenance of friendship. According to Josephine M. Ford, *"Lysis shows that friendship is superior to love because it guarantees better the interpersonal characteristics of stability and faithfulness."* [53]

Aristotle

Aristotle sees friendship as either being a virtue itself or as involving virtue which leads to *eudaimonia*. According to Aristotle, "*eudaimonia* is especially the most end not simply because it meets the *haplos television* (complete without qualification) *requirement* but also because pleasure, intellectual wisdom, and the moral virtues are choice worthy for its sake."[54] Lorraine Smith Page elaborates on what Aristotle intends to teach about friendship. She claims:

> *"Friendship now comes to sight as a third and perhaps highest summit of the moral life, on which virtue and happiness may finally be united. If the life of a great-souled man lacks clear content, if putting himself in the service of his inferiors seemed lavish, and if actions aimed at winning honor from*

> *them seem undignified, the pursuit of serious friendship is a worthy outlet for his energies and talents. Friendship likewise completes and goes beyond justice, or even renders justice unnecessary. The goodness shown in noble friendship seems higher than justice, not only because its object is so worthy but because it is entirely dependent on one's character and choice and is not defined and compelled by law."* 55

Aristotle identifies friendship as a necessity for a good life and a choice people make if they live together in a community. Aristotle discusses three forms of friendship: friendship based on pleasure, utility, and virtue (friendship involving persons and not things).

Aristotle acknowledges goodwill as a principle that makes it possible for two people to go beyond the theoretical possibility of establishing friendship to being friends. In other words, goodwill is a potential friendship that arises from virtue, and not on account of pleasure or utility. Friendship on account of pleasure or utility is not durable, since conflicts or challenges of some sort can easily break such friendship. Only friends of virtue have the potency for durability; only friends of virtue form a real friendship. Aristotle argues that only friendship of virtue is capable of reciprocity. In his words,

"Hence the friendship of base people turns out to be vicious for they are unstable and share base pursuits; and by becoming like each other, they grow vicious. But the friendship of decent people is decent and increases the more often they meet. And they seem to become still better from their activities and their mutual correction. Each molds the other in what they approve of so that you will learn what is noble from noble people." [56]

Cicero

Cicero acknowledges that we encounter people and, in most cases, treat them as friends. This is the case with business associates, colleagues, classmates, or playmates. He goes further to distinguish between these acquaintances and those to whom we truly bind ourselves at a deeper level. This second group of people is rare because relatedness with this group requires commitment and intentionality. Even more, such relatedness requires personal goodness. According to Philip Freeman, who comments on Cicero's *Decmicitia*,

"Only good people can be true friends: people of poor moral character can have friends but can only be friends of utility because real friendship requires trust, wisdom, and basic goodness. Tyrants and scoundrels can use each other, just as they

can use good people, but bad people can never find real friendships in life." [57]

One cannot give what one does not have. True friendship is not interested in a person because of what one can gain. Cicero acknowledges that friendship is somehow divine, as C. W. Earle quotes:

"Now friendship may be thus defined: a complete accord on all subjects, human and divine, joined with mutual goodwill and affection. And except wisdom, I am inclined to think nothing better than this has been given to man by the immortal gods." [58]

In a discussion with Fannius, Scaevola, and Laelius on friendship in the book *Treatise on Friendship and Old Age*, Cicero reports Laelius' comments on the distinguishing factors involving friendship: Now friendship may be thus defined: a complete accord on all subjects, human and divine, joined with mutual goodwill and affection. And except for wisdom, I am inclined to think nothing better than this has been given to man by the immortal gods. Some people give the palm to riches, good health, power, office, and even sensual pleasures. This last is the ideal of brute beasts, and of the others, we may say that they are frail and uncertain and depend less on our prudence than on the caprice of fortune.[59]

For Cicero, friendship seeks virtue as the foundation of the relationship and honors the dignity of the person as a good to be pursued. This type of friendship comes with its blessings and makes it possible for people to flourish.

Augustine on Friendship

Augustine is platonic regarding love's possibilities. But he was also a devotee of the stoic philosophy of Cicero, Seneca, and Marcus Aurelius. Augustine develops his discussions on friendship from the Stoics' interpretation of love, friendship, and passion. According to Marcia L. Colish,

> *"For the Stoics, true friendship is a relationship between the wise, wisdom, and virtue being prerequisites for it. Friends enjoy a perfect meeting of minds, sharing the same values and goals and enriching each other's lives in a completely nonexploitative way. Friendship is a freely chosen state reflecting a delight in rational companionship; it is not a means of gratifying or expressing man's instinctual needs"*.[60]

Augustine believes that disordered love also pulls us away from true friendship and God. Augustine argues that love is typically disordered because of concupiscence. He argues that the remedy to our present human predicament and abuse of love and friendship is not to cease love but rather to rediscover how to love authentically. Augustine emphasizes that without peace within the individual, the individual will be incapable of befriending himself, which puts the bond of friendship between two people in a difficult position.

Augustine, following Neo-Platonists, understands friendship as basic to education and the improvement of human beings, which makes it a necessary part of human flourishing. Augustine adopts several insights from Platonism to buttress this point. According to Augustine, "The friendship which draws human beings together in a tender bond is sweet to us because out of many minds, it forges a unity."[61] The goal of friendship is to seek God.[62] Donald X. Burt remarks,

> *"On earth, this expansion [from immanent to transcendent] is necessarily imperfect and limited but hints at the heavenly city's perfect and infinite friendship once its membership is fixed beyond time. This uniting love affords a glimpse of what is to come. It is also the way to that blessed state. The peacemakers of this world will finally enjoy the perfect peace of union with God. Then there will no longer be alienation. There will be only love."*[63]

Man and woman through their friendship though imperfect still express that possibility of friendship with God. Kim Paffenroth writes

> *"true friendship is, in short, one of the strongest experiences one can have of oneself and another human being as the image of God, simultaneous with one of the strongest experiences of oneself and the friend as vulnerable, fallen creatures. These two sides of the experience and human nature, each so intensely and completely true, are what give friendship its overwhelming and transformative power, teaching and showing us who we are."* [64]

Augustine argues that true friendship is a bond established by Christ through love and enlightened by the Holy Spirit. He makes a distinction between a friendship that results from a long period of acquittance and friendship that is made possible because of mutual recognition of the right faith through the presence and power of the Holy Spirit. Augustine remarks, "Friendship is genuine only when you bind fast together people who cleave to you through the charity poured in our hearts by the Holy Spirit who is given to us."[65] According to Paul Helm, Augustine recounting the impact of the death of his friend, remarks, "It was less than true friendship which is not possible unless you bond together those who cleave by the love."[66]

Augustine calls any friendship that takes one away from the good and distorts the love that is the foundation of friendship *unfriendly friendship*. For instance, he sees "sexual transgressions and theft for theft's sake, sharing the same root: misapplied friendship."[67] Friendship seeks a higher good altogether. It ceases to be authentic if it does not lead to a life of grace and holiness. Friends wish and encourage each other in a life of grace here on earth and make possible transcendent movement toward heaven. True friendship predicts new perspectives and possibilities for two friends. According to Augustine, "The sincerity of our friendship should ensure that this thing should not belong to one person, and that, to another, there would be one single property formed out of many; the whole would belong to each of us, and all things would belong to all."[68]

Paul Waddell argues that, for Augustine, love in friendship is, at its best, a function of divine relatedness. Waddell writes;

> *"Augustine saw Christian friendship envisioning a different possibility. In Christian friendships, he believed, each friend wishes for the other a life of holiness and grace on earth and everlasting happiness with God and the saints in heaven. Of course, the good that friends*

seek for one another would also include well-being and happiness in this world, but the primary aim of benevolence in Christian friendships, Augustine believed, was to help one's friends grow in the new life of grace. To seek what is best for one's friends was not only to help them make their way in the world but also to help them make their way to the reign of God and the communion of saints. The friends would not want one another to lose sight of their life's greatest hope and possibility. Augustine's friends sought happiness and well-being for one another in a life of holiness on earth and beatitude in heaven. It is friendship informed by a different narrative vision, a vision that ultimately presents a very different understanding of the friendship's purpose and perfection. In the Christian narrative, friendships give us companionship on earth, but their ultimate purpose is to help us gain companionship with God, angels, and the saints in heaven." [69]

For Augustine, friendship is a school through which we learn to love, practice love, and grow in the perfection of love and life. Augustine teaches that God is the *summum bonum* (highest good); every other love must be about God. Waddell remarks,

"Since God is the source of all goodness, the source of all that we love, all our loves should be directed to God. This is precisely the point. If we direct all our love to God,

> *including our love for our friends, then friendship does not compete with our love for God but expresses and deepens it. Augustine did not want our wholehearted love for God to require a halfhearted love for our friends."* [70]

Augustine reiterates that our authentic love for God is manifest in how true our friendship with each other becomes. This does not diminish our friendship with each other; rather, it enhances our friendship. Friendship becomes essential to encounter God and grow mutually in his love. For Augustine, "Friendship becomes a kind of sacrament, a vital sign of God's active and personal love for us and our active and very personal love for God."[71] Friendship understood in this perspective develops a strong sense of intimacy and unity that transforms two people in spirit and soul.

Augustine significantly explores the relationship between friendship and marriage, identifying both as goods in themselves. In *De Bono Coniugali,* Augustine comments:

> *"I do not believe that marriage is good solely because of the procreation of children: there is also the natural association (societas) between the sexes. Otherwise, we would no longer speak of a marriage between elderly people, especially if they had lost or had never produced*

> *children. But now, in a good marriage, even if it has lasted for many years and even if the youthful ardor between the male and female has faded, the order of charity between husband and wife still thrives."* [72]

The bond of friendship is central to marriage; therefore, procreation is not the sole reason for marriage. There is also the bond of unity that true friendship establishes, and which serves as a *teleos* of marriage.[73]

Aquinas on Friendship

Aquinas built on the legacy of Augustine, also expanding in depth Aristotle's treatise on friendship. Aquinas, in the *Summa Theologiae,* provides an insight into the mutuality of friendship as follows,

> *"Since friendship involves mutuality, there must be reciprocity; this implies communication, which means that I cannot be friends with people who fail to acknowledge my friendship by not communicating their acceptance in words or actions. This condition incidentally also signifies that friendship constitutes a particular form of goodness specified by recognizing that the friendly overture is acceptable."* [74]

For Aquinas, friends share something in common, and that which they share leads to a higher goal. It is necessary to remark here that "the friend intends an association or sharing based on his affection for the good of the other person; his goal is to preserve both what is common and what unifies himself and his friend."[75] He identifies true friendship as one that does not use another as if one is an inanimate object. Friendship always pursues the common good, and when it becomes inimical to the common good, it becomes something else other than friendship. Aquinas believes that friendship exists for a higher value other than itself, and hence, friendship sought for the sake of the good is a virtue. Aquinas disagrees with Albert the Great's view that "friendship is secondary or annexed intellectual virtue perfecting reason in its tendency toward another person and, as such, results from the possession of other virtues. He agrees with Aristotle that friendship is not a virtue, but an effect of virtue, that is, with virtue for the act of friendship includes a mutual return of love, while a virtuous act is only the act of one person".[76] Friendship as actuation of virtue is often seen as higher than friendship for the sake of pleasure or utility, but friendship for the sake of virtue contains elements of pleasure and utility.

Aquinas also argues that friendship is not an act based on feeling but a habit, a virtue based on choice. Aquinas refers to that love that brings friends together as *Dilectio*. *Dilectio* is defined as *"love that involves choice."* [77] Bernard V. Brady writes,

> *"Love unites. Thomas knows this from experience, and thus he offers some strong and interesting words on friendship. He believes the bonds of true friendship are so strong that the friend becomes like another self. He writes: when a man loves another with the love of friendship, he wills good to him, just as he wills good to himself: wherefore he apprehends him as his other self, in so far, to wit as he wills good to him as to himself. Hence a friend is called a man's other self."* [78]

Aquinas teaches that the mystery of the Incarnation is intrinsically Trinitarian. According to Dominic Legge,

> *"Aquinas formulates a distinctively Trinitarian insight: exitus and reditus account for how the Trinitarian processions themselves ground both creation and the Trinitarian dispensation of grace. This is an original contribution of St. Thomas, and he used it to explain the scriptural and Patristic teaching that we return to the Father through the missions of the Son and the Holy Spirit. As Thomas puts it, 'Just as we were created through the Son and the Holy Spirit, likewise we also are joined [through them] to our ultimate end."* [79]

Aquinas understands God as so transcendent, so beyond the creation of even what humans can imagine, that there isn't much we can know about him without His revelation to us.

Incarnation As an Expression of Friendship

The Incarnation, Aquinas argues, "is most fitting as it is according to supreme goodness of the Divine nature that he communicates himself."[80] As a result of the human friendship that serves as a form and goal of marriage, Christians discover the possibility of genuine friendship with God. This is made possible by God's choice in the Incarnation. Moreover, the Incarnation Aquinas affirms is most fitting as it relates to the human virtue of friendship and friendship's experience by grace; this idea helps Christians to reflect on their relationship, which is possible through the incarnation.

Before the Incarnation, God was far away and distant from human experience, with the result that our relationship with the all-powerful God was best described as "fear of the Lord." With Incarnation, as God becomes present in human form, the distance between God and the human community is flattened out, and our relationship can become of love in friendship. Scripture says, "I no longer call you slaves because a slave does not know what his master is doing. I have called you friends because I have told you everything I have heard from my father". [81] Aquinas points out how the incarnation makes possible a relationship with God that can be characterized as friendship.

Waddell writes, "The core of relationship for Thomas is a friendship with God that captures the most profoundly promising possibility of our lives. We are called through love to be for God who God has always been for us a friend, a source of happiness and delight, one who is key to the other person's joy."[82] The friendship that human beings share with God is not made possible by mere human endeavor. In Aquinas' words, "Now thus, the fellowship of [the human] with God, which consists in a certain familiar colloquy with him, is begun here in this in this life, by grace, but will be perfected in the future life, by glory"[83] In God, we see perfectly how we love people and find friendship possible in the mind of God to whom all friendship leads.

The Incarnation is a perfect expression of the third form of friendship that Aristotle spoke about, namely, the friendship of virtue, characterized as a kind of love that seeks the good. Fulton Sheen provides an insight into such love as follows.

> *"In erotic or selfish love, the burdens of others are regarded as impeding one's happiness. But in Christian love, burdens become opportunities to serve. That is why the symbol of Christian love is not a circle, circumscribed by self, but the cross, with*

its arms outstretched to infinity to embrace all humanity within its grasp. But despite love's best effort, there is no control over a partner." [84]

Incarnation is selfless, with the cross as the perfect symbol. Through the power of the Holy Spirit, the Church is responsible for communicating the realities and possibilities of the Incarnation to the world.

Chapter Four
Friendship and Marriage

Since a man and a woman can make a personal choice to establish a relationship of friendship, marriage can signify a Christian relationship with God. A marriage built on friendship flourishes with faith and trust, testifying to the reality of universal communion with God within the companionship of married love. Burt writes,

> *"One of the reasons that faith and trust are necessary for human affairs is because without them, friendship is impossible, and without friendship, marriage is impossible. Marriage does not depend on a couple's ability to propagate; rather, it depends on their ability and willingness to be one in the heart. Good marriage brings to the human race, and the spouses are not restricted to the children that may be produced. It also includes the natural companionship of husband and wife."* [85]

The Sacrament of Marriage is one of the ways to witness that brand of love expressed on the cross for us, who are the friends of God.

Aquinas argues that marriage is the appropriate venue for coitus and reproduction. For him, "sexual intercourse is proper, and by reason, as long as it is open to conception."[86] The proper activity of man is not independent of reason, and for this reason, it led him to the consideration for the necessity of friendship in marriage. He claims that the indissoluble nature of marriage is vital not because of reproduction but for companionship.

Aquinas addresses polyandry and polygamy. Polyandry is wrongful because it is difficult, sometimes impossible, to determine the father of a child. Thomas also insists that polygamy is wrong because it creates inequality, especially in marriage. Aquinas says, "If a wife has but one husband, but the husband has several wives, the friendship will not be equal on both sides. So, the friendship will not be free, but servile in some way."[87] In this way, Aquinas treats marriage as a *vita domestica* that is more than a business arrangement about children: it is about friendship, not just about baby-making. Marriage is not just about pleasure; neither is it just about utility. Friendship is beyond pleasure and utility. Aquinas agrees with Aristotle, who identifies three types of friendship: pleasure, utility, and virtue. Only friendship of virtue can establish and sustain a marriage. Aristotle says thus of friendship:

> *"Those who love for utility or pleasure, then, are fond of a friend because of what is good or pleasant for themselves, not insofar as the beloved is who he is, but insofar as he is useful or pleasant. Hence these friendships, as well as the friends, are coincidental since the beloved is loved not insofar as he is who he is but insofar as he provides some good or pleasure."* [88]

Friendship is also cemented by sex, and more so, the friendship of marriage implies indissolubility. In Aquinas' words, *"There seems to be the greatest friendship between husband and wife because they are united not only in the act of carnal union, which produces a certain gentle association even among beasts but also in the partnership of the whole range of domestic activity."* [89]

Marriage involves pleasure, but that is not all. Aquinas argues that sexual pleasure can be an offense either as a fixation or as a defective appropriation of sexual pleasure, which he calls "insensibility." Sexual impropriety is not only animalistic but is a lack of appreciation of the joy of sex. For Aquinas, however, there is also the evil doppelganger of chastity, which under-appreciates the natural sensory pleasures of life. In Aquinas' words,

> *"Nature has introduced pleasure into the issues needed for human life. Thus, the natural order requires one should make use of pleasures in so far as they are necessary for human well-being, as regards either the preservation of the individual or the preservation of the species. Accordingly, if one were to reject pleasure to the extent of omitting things that are necessary for nature's preservation, he would sin, acting counter to the natural order. And this pertains to the vice of insensibility."* [90]

Whereas Augustine sees friendship as the *telos* of marriage, Aquinas addresses friendship as a *sine-qua-non,* the forma the DNA of marriage. He further explains this by referencing the marriage of Mary and Joseph. In Aquinas's words, *"Thus we may say, as to the first perfection, that the marriage of the Virgin Mother of God and Joseph was true: because both consented to the nuptial bond, but not expressly to the bond of the flesh, save on condition that it was pleasing to God."* [91] As it regards to no sex as in the case of Mary and Joseph, Aquinas reminds us that *"the form of matrimony consists in a certain inseparable union of souls, by which husband and wife are pledged by a bond of mutual affection that cannot be broken apart."* [92]

Aquinas sees true friendship as a union in which both friends work for mutual growth, and none loses oneself. In Aquinas' words, "he who loves, goes out from himself, in so far as he wills the good of his friend and works for it. Yet he does not will the good of his friend more than his good; and so, it does not follow that he loves another more than himself"[93] Authentic friendship must be mutual and largely selfless. Friendship begins with a choice but extends beyond choice because "friendship is mutual and depends on the mutual assent of each person. It rests on my choice but is ultimately beyond my choice."[94] Human friendship has practical meaning for Aquinas in terms of marriage. Therefore, Aquinas, friendship is the *forma*, the *DNA* of marriage. In his words,

> *"Marriage or wedlock is said to be true because of it attaining its perfection. Now perfection of anything is twofold; first and second. The first perfection of a thing consists in its form, from which it receives its species, while the second perfection of a thing consists in its operation, by which in some way a thing attains its end. Now the form of matrimony consists of a certain inseparable union of souls, by which husband and wife are pledged by a bond of mutual affection that cannot be sundered. And the end of matrimony is the begetting and upbringing of children: the first of which is attained by conjugal intercourse; the second by the other duties of husband and wife, by which they help one another in rearing their offspring."* [95]

Chapter Five
The Pastoral Application in the Marriage Preparation Process

Marriage as Part of Human Society

Marriage has always been about establishing a permanent relationship between a man and a woman for an exclusive domestic and sexual union. It is necessary to note that marriage is more than a man and a woman coming together for procreation. Marriage is a socio-legal institution involving such issues as tenants by entireties, inheritance, and surname change typically on the part of the woman. Marriage as a social phenomenon also entails a legal binding on each party through the issuance of the marriage license and the fact that one party cannot just walk away from the union but must follow a legal process to be freed from the bond of the relationship. The USCCB document on marriage writes, "Marriage does not exist solely for the reproduction of another member of the species but for the creation of a communion of persons."[96] Marriage is not for the begetting of children who live as monads but for persons in relationships and interaction with others in society.

The marriage preparation sessions must help the engaged couples understand that emotions and subjective individual experiences do not sustain the socio-legal commitment required in a marital union, especially when situations challenge their promise to each other to be there "in sickness and in health", and in "richness and in poverty." When pastoral ministers fail to include human formation and growth in marriage preparation sessions, they fail to adequately prepare couples to remain stable and committed amid inevitable storms of life that they might face in their marriage. A proposed outline for the session must see marriage as a phenomenon of human society and the base of a civic community.

Marriage as Part of Ecclesial Society

Marriage is part of ecclesial society: it is not simply between individuals but has clear ecclesial effects. Marriage requires ecclesial oversight for the couple to enter marriage; it does not usually permit a couple to separate or divorce on their authority; the Church regulates the entirety of marriage in the Code of Canon Law. Marriage is the foundation of society, and through the family, society is sustained. Thus, even more, marriage is part of ecclesial society.

Marriage is constituted by mutual consent between a man and a woman, which gives rise to claims and responsibilities. When we speak of marriage as a covenant, we think of a covenant "in its normal sense, an elected, as opposed to natural, the relationship of an obligation under oath."[97] Married life and intimate partnerships are established by God and have the law's backing. Michael G. Lawler quotes *The Code of Canon Law* canon 1055, which clearly describes marriage as a covenant. The Code states that the "marriage covenant by which a man and a woman establish between themselves a partnership of their whole life, and which of its very nature is ordered to the well-being of the spouses and the procreation and upbringing of children, has, between the baptized, been raised by Christ the Lord to the dignity of a sacrament."[98] Marriage raised to the dignity of a sacrament is more than just the gift of grace; it also becomes a public act of worship on the part of the Church.[99]

In preparing engaged couples, pastoral ministers must tell them that responsibility entails mutual consent freely exchanged with each other. Consent establishes marriage, and any significant defects in the exchange of consent or the capacity of each to give or accept consent make the union invalid. Consent must be thoughtful, cognitive, and volitional. It is necessary to help the couple appreciate that "marriage involves faith; it is a sacrament, an act of worship, an expression of faith, a sign of the Church's unity and a witness to the presence of Christ."[100]

The effectiveness of marriage in Catholic ecclesial society also takes cognizance of the canonical form. Canon 1117 in the Code exempted persons who had left the Church by the formal act from the obligation of canonical form. *Ominium In Mentem* by Benedict XVI changed this returning to Trent's *Tamesti* decree at the stipulations of the 1917 *Code*. Omnium *In Mentem* revised the stipulation of Canon 1117 and decreed that all who were baptized a Catholic or who became Catholic are bound to canonical form. In the words of Pope Benedict XVI,

> *"The Code of Canon Law nonetheless prescribes that the faithful who have left the Church 'by a formal act' are not bound by the ecclesiastical laws regarding the canonical form of marriage (cf. can. 1117), a dispensation from the impediment of disparity of cult (cf. can. 1086) and the need for permission in the case of mixed marriages (cf. can. 1124). The underlying aim of this exception from the general norm of can. 11 was to ensure that marriages contracted by faithful members would not be invalid due to defect of form or the impediment of disparity of cult."* [101]

The sacrament is a universal phenomenon within the Universal Church as Pope Benedict XVI, being the competent authority to legislate on the validity of the sacraments, clarifies what canonical form entails in our present time: the sacrament of marriage as a universal phenomenon within the Universal Church.

> *"The engaged couples receive instruction regarding the natural requirements of the interpersonal relationship between a man and a woman in God's plan for marriage and the family: awareness regarding freedom of consent as the foundation of their union, the unity and indissolubility of marriage, the correct concept of responsible parenthood, the human aspects of conjugal sexuality, the conjugal act with its requirements and ends, and the proper education of children. All of this aims to know the moral truth and form a personal conscience."* [102]

The couple is entering a juridic reality that manifests a covenantal reality. Pope St. John Paul II explains in *Familiaris Consortio* that in marriage, *"the spouses participate in it as spouses, together, as a couple, so that the first and immediate effect of marriage (res et sacramentum) is not supernatural grace itself, but the Christian conjugal bond, a typically Christian communion of two persons because it represents the mystery of Christ's incarnation and the mystery of his covenant."* [103] *Through this free giving and receiving, they are "now joined in 'holy covenant', each spouse having the right to receive conjugal love, a love that is faithful, permanent, and open to having and raising children together, which includes the right to sexual intercourse."* [104] This mutual intimacy expressed through the conjugal love of spouses extends the couples' participation in the larger Church's life as nourished and sustained by the redemptive power of Christ. In the words of Burke-Sivers,

> *"Through the power of Christ's redemptive death, which is both actualized in the Eucharist and symbolized in the marriage covenant, the husband and wife as a domestic church, as an intimate community of conjugal life and love, and as the quintessential incarnation of the larger Church are elevated and assumed into the spousal charity of Christ, sustained, and enriched by His redeeming power."* [105]

This necessary insight proposes why marriage is a public ministry in the service of the larger Church as a testimony of God's fidelity and love for His Church. In the words of Pope John Paul II:

> *"Spouses are, therefore, the permanent reminder to the Church of what happened on the Cross; they are for one another and*

the children witnesses to the salvation in which the sacrament makes them sharers. Of this salvation event, marriage, like every sacrament, is a memorial, actuation, and prophecy: as a memorial, the sacrament gives them the grace and duty of commemorating the great works of God and of bearing witness to them before their children. Actuation gives them the grace and duty of putting into practice in the present, towards each other and their children, the demands of a love that forgives and redeems. As prophecy, it gives them the grace and duty of living and bearing witness to the hope of a future encounter with Christ." [106]

Marriage is objectively seen as a sacrament of Christ, and His Church is indissoluble. Aquinas based *"The indissolubility of marriage on the fact that it is a sacrament of the indissoluble bond of Christ and His Church."* [107]

Marriage as a Liturgical Event

Pastoral ministers need to emphasize that the Church is a community in which the presence and power of God of creation and covenant are felt manifested in three actions: *martyria, leitourgia, and Diakonia.* It is crucial to note that *"The Church's deepest nature is expressed in her three-fold responsibility: of proclaiming the word of God (kerygma-martyria), celebrating the sacraments (leitourgia), and exercising the ministry of charity (diakonia). These duties presuppose each other and are inseparable. For the Church, charity is not a kind of welfare activity but is a part of her nature, an indispensable expression of her very being."* [108] The Eucharist is the highest form through which Catholic Christians express their praise and worship. The Church has come to understand that marriage itself, in addition to being a door for grace, is also a vehicle for giving praise and worship to God in and through the presence and power of Jesus Christ.

The idea of the presence and power of God in the assembled community is part of the fund of convictions common to Judaism and Christianity. The Church, as the Body of Christ, lives in the presence of God; God dwells with his people through the presence and power of the Holy Spirit. That the assembled community initiates the presence of God is not the Christian conception of divine worship, nor is it the Catholic notion of the liturgy. This presence is caused by divine initiative. For Christians, it is always mediated presence; it always requires a 'medium' that is highly perceptible. But the goal is always the same: a mediated presence that results in genuine, grace-filled, personal communication between human beings and God. Using the liturgy, we do not make God the Father present to us. Rather, it is we who, in and using the liturgy, is made present to God the Father, and are brought through and with and in his Son Jesus in the Holy Spirit. [109]

Pope Benedict XVI has placed this into the context of the Church as the Body of Christ, a Eucharistic community in which we are invited to participate. As participants in Christ's body, the married couple gives praise and worship to the Father of Jesus. Pope Benedict XVI writes, "This transformation is possible thanks to a communion stronger than division, the communion of God himself. The word 'communion,' which we also use to designate the Eucharist, in itself sums up the vertical and horizontal dimensions of Christ's gift" [110] Through marriage,

> *"Marital intimacy and the good of the children require total fidelity to conjugal love. This flows from Christ's fidelity to the Church, which he loved so much that he died for her. By their mutual fidelity, the spouses continue to make presentations to each other about the love of Christ and lead each other to greater holiness through the grace they receive from the Sacrament."* [111]

Married couples, by their participation in the community life of the Church, expressed in a concrete manner the love that God has for his church;

> *"Spouses encounter the love that animates and sustains their marriage, the love of*

> *Christ for his Church. The encounter enables them to perceive that their marriage and family are not isolated units but that they are to reach out in love to the broader Church and world in which they are living. Marriage continually sends the believing Catholic back again to the Eucharist. Here is where the gratitude that has become a life-giving habit in a marriage can be fully and completely expressed."* [112]

Marriage invites the married couple to participate in the life and mission of the church as a worshiping community. It is necessary to state that,

> *"Alive in the tradition of the Church and deepened by the Magisterium, the Word of God stresses that marriage for Christian spouses implies a response to God's vocation and the acceptance of the mission to be a sign of God's love for all the members of the human family, by partaking in the definitive covenant of Christ with the Church. Therefore, spouses become cooperators with the Creator and Savior in the gift of love and life. Hence Christian marriage preparation is described as a journey of faith that does not end with the celebration of marriage but continues through family life. Therefore, our perspective does not close with marriage as an act at the moment of its celebration but is ongoing."* [113]

Familiaris Consortio puts it this way:

> *"The very preparation for Christian marriage is itself a journey of faith. It is a special opportunity for the engaged to rediscover and deepen the faith received in Baptism and nourished by their Christian upbringing. In this way, they come to recognize and freely accept their vocation to follow Christ and serve God's kingdom in the married state."* [114]

The sacrament of marriage is a witness to divine love and fidelity and is lived in the context of a worship-directed call within the Church as the Body of Christ. Moreover, married couples must see their union as participation in the Church as the Sacrament of Christ in which salvation in God's life is offered, and praise and thanksgiving to the Father of Jesus are enacted.[115] Our praise and worship are shown forth and made present in a particular way by the participation of married couples in their marital covenant. According to the *United States Catholic Catechism for Adults*,

> *"The couple witnesses Christ's spousal love for the Church through their marriage. One of the Nuptial Blessings in the liturgical celebration of marriage refers to this in saying, 'Father, you have made the union of man and wife*

> *so holy a mystery that symbolizes the marriage of Christ and his Church.' Through the liturgical celebration of marriage, husband, and wife enter a covenant which is also a sacrament."* [116]

Marriage and its Theological Implications

Pastoral ministers need to insist that marriage must be open to the possibility not just of "reproduction" but also of procreation, opening 'to be' spouses to the opportunity to become procreators with God. Even more, Pastoral ministers need to show that marriage is not only about procreation but also about friendship. Marriage is a union of love and procreation in which a man and a woman establish a relationship between themselves, a spiritual, emotional, and physical friendship.

The sacrament of marriage, as a sacrament of praise and worship, manifests the fact that marriage, expressed in its openness to the possibility of procreation, buttresses God's creative act. Even more, marriage discloses and presents God's love and a couple's grateful human response. Thus, the majority of theologians view marriage as *"the best paradigm of a sacrament, deeply rooted as it is in the human and concrete yet taken over and transformed by the love of God."* [117] The spouses, through their love for each other, become sacramental ministers to each other, expressing the totality and fidelity of God's love for his people and an adequate human response in Christ to this faithful love. The marital love between a husband and wife can truly become a means and a sign of God's first creation and second creation and a grateful response for such divine gifts. Marriage makes concrete the possibility of our friendship toward God made accessible in the Incarnate Word. According to Vorgrimler, "In a specifically Catholic conception, the history of God with humanity has a sacramental structure, in the sense that the movement proceeding from God, and through the whole course of human history, returning to God is continually taking on more precisely sacramental characteristics."[118] Marriage establishes that context in which the encounter of the friendship between the spouses made possible by the Holy Spirit draws them to offer praise and worship in and through their friendship in Christ.

Christian marriage is more than a union of a man and a woman. Lawler argues, "*A Christian marriage is intentionally more than just the communion for the whole of life of this man and this woman. It is more than just a human covenant: it is also a religious covenant. It is more than law, obligations, and rights; it is also grace.*" [119]

According to the *National Directory for Catechesis*,

> "*Human experiences provide the sensible signs that lead the person, by the grace of the Holy Spirit, to a better*

understanding of the truths of the faith. They are the means through which human beings come to know themselves, one another, and God. They give rise to concerns and questions, hopes and anxieties, reflections, and judgments, increasing one's desire to penetrate deeper into life's meaning. Human experience serves to examine and accept the truths contained in the deposit of revelation." [120]

What has been said earlier in this treatise bears repeating. According to Donald Burt, "Augustine maintained that the essential characteristic of a valid marriage is that it be a union of friends, a friendship solidified by fidelity to one's spouse and the permanence of the commitment. One can have friends without getting married, but the bond of friendship between those who are married is of a special kind."[121] Aquinas speaks of the marriage of Mary and Joseph as a union of souls. In his own words, "the marriage of the Virgin Mother of God and Joseph was true: because both consented to the nuptial bond, but not expressly to the bond of the flesh, save on the condition that is was pleasing to God."[122] Friendship in marriage brings in concrete terms our friendship with God in Christ and shows the quality of love we share. In marriage, "the true test for the sacramental character of a marriage lies in the quality of the love found in the relationship."[123]

By the Incarnation, by God's own choice, there is a flattening of divine transcendence, which enables humans to relate to God in friendship, not just in fear of the Lord. The Incarnation of Christ makes possible a connection between the couple's friendship with each other and their friendship with God.

Ministers often overlook friendship when we prepare people for the sacrament of marriage. We tend to focus on logistics, which is important. Still, we fail to explore with the engaged couple how what they are about to establish is a testimony to the possibility of friendship with God through the Incarnate Word. Moreover, the love in marriage can actuate the transcendental possibility of God's Incarnational friendship with the spouses. This is to say; marriage is a sign and instrument of friendship with God, a sacrament of friendship with God. Moreover, this sacramentality is both 'low' sacramentality, by which the couple wishes a friendship with God, and 'high' sacramentality, by which God becomes present in friendship to the spouses.

Faith in the sacramental reality of marriage enables a couple to incluturate a sense of communion in the Body of Christ. Married couples embrace a conversion from the enculturation of expressive individualism in our culture to an inculturation of Christian fidelity of love and care of love that overrides the expressive individualism that undermines marital fidelity. The four considerations discussed in this chapter are needed in presenting an adequate marriage preparation. How best to incorporate these four considerations is beyond the scope of this study since every diocese and parish is unique, and their needs differ. We need to have a preparation process that does not overlook the human formation of the engaged couples and the need for them to understand their union as witnesses and instruments of the possibility of our friendship with God.

Marriage begins as a human choice and natural institution and becomes a privileged avenue through which married couples offer praise and worship to God. Marriage as a covenant that is considered a divine gift discloses the first creation and the new creation of a faithful, loving God.

Finally, friendship becomes the DNA of marriage, testifying that the possibility of our friendship with God is made possible through the Incarnation of Christ.

Chapter 6
Catechumenate as a Model:

We may be wondering why the whole emphasis is on a reevaluation of marriage preparation. This answer is so simple, times have changed, and society has become more diverse with its accompanying challenges. The marriage challenge today is more complex than it was in the past. Today many marriages fail and end in divorce or separation or even in some form of compromise. If marriage must retain its noble stance and remain a vocation as well as a sacrament, we must do better in preparing and supporting engaged couples. In this chapter, I shall look at how marriage preparation can be enhanced using the catechumenate models to help people appreciate and understand the true meaning of sacramental marriage. The United States continues to be more diverse, which comes with challenges and must be addressed with new tools and processes. The catechumenate model provides those tools that treat the sacrament as something that is individually received but publicly witnessed.

I also will look at some of the ways marriage preparations happen and the tools out there while providing insights into how these tools can be helpful in the time and recommend a couple of mentor programs to balance the clergy role with the role the faithful play in ensuring the success of engaged couples while providing support to them.

Marriage Catechumenate

Marriage is one of the vital sacraments and because of a series of attacks, it needs a process that aids the engaged couples in understanding the seriousness of the obligation they are to take upon themselves. The catechumenate model becomes an exemplary process that provides a such platform and creates an opportunity for the couples and the parish community to engage in the process. The *National Directory for Catechesis* presents the baptismal catechumenate as "the source of inspiration for all catechesis."[124] The baptismal catechumenate treats the sacraments as a journey of conversion and growth as individuals and a faith community. It is "both a process of formation and a true school of the faith."[125] The process helps the engaged couples to deepen their faith gradually and comprehend intentionally the mysteries they are to undertake.

The increase in divorce and cohabitation makes it necessary that engaged couples be prepared well enough to deepen their knowledge, clarify, and affirm their faith so that they appreciate what they are to undertake. Fintan Gavin provides an elaborate explanation of what this preparation modeled after the catechumenate looks like. According to Gavin, "this preparation is described as a catechumenate for Christian marriage involving instruction in the following areas: the interpersonal relationship of man and woman, conjugal sexuality, responsible parenthood, essential biological knowledge, domestic economy, that is steady work, finance, housekeeping details, and so forth, education of children, membership, and involvement in the family apostolate of the Church."[126] The Catechumenate process creates the opportunity to address the demands of the sacrament and to help the engaged couples fully understand the mystery's beauty while building trust that they are not alone on the journey. To unpack the realities surrounding the sacramental marriage, there is a need for enough process and time to provide new insight and form to the pre-nuptial inquiry and assessment used by the parish or diocese. The catechumenate offers even more opportunity for the engaged couples to progress at their own pace, especially for those who are struggling with their faith, have doubts, or are reluctant to embrace what the Church teaches. The purpose of the process must be "to lead the couple to a deeper knowledge of the mystery of Christ and the Church, of the meaning of grace and the responsibility of Christian marriage."[127]

The catechumenate also involves the preparation of the rituals of the sacrament to get the couples ready to participate actively in the celebration consciously and intentionally. It also creates an opportunity for "the entire ecclesial community to involve itself in the preparation of the young people for marriage."[128] Each parish is unique and must work these general principles to suit the faithful and meet their needs. It is necessary to pay attention to the context of the faith community so that the process is not just intellectual but structured so that the engaged couples feel the desire and courage to involve themselves in parish life actively. Pope Francis invites the priests to get involved in the process and not abandon it to delegates. According to Pope Francis, "the Church's pastors are not only responsible for promoting Christian marriage but also the "discernment of the situations of a great many who no longer live with this reality."[129] The catechumenate provides that platform that allows the freedom to discern and not to assume that the engaged couples understand what they are asking. It makes it possible for the priest to know if the couples need more time or need to work on something. This is important, especially when young people are afraid to make a long-lasting commitment and when culture encourages expressive individualism as opposed to freedom with responsibility; most people want to be free yet enjoy the benefits without any commitment, so people prefer to cohabit.

The Church in a diverse society like the United States pays attention to the impact these diversities have on the preparation process of the sacrament. The Church must respond to these changes in an appropriate manner that does not threaten the people who are coming up for the sacrament but in a way that accompanies them to embrace the obligations of the sacrament freely and joyfully. The admonition of Pope John 11 in *Familiaris Consortio* is much more appropriate today; he remarks that "more than ever necessary in our times is the preparation of young people for marriage and family. In some countries, it is still the families that, according to ancient customs, ensure the passing on to young people of the values concerning marriage and family life, and they do this through a gradual process of education or initiation. But the changes that have taken place within almost all modern societies demand that the family, society, and the Church should be involved in properly preparing young people for their future responsibilities."[130] Preparation for the sacrament of marriage must not be rushed, and nothing needs to be overlooked; it must be approached as a process and not an event, for it continues even after the celebration of the sacrament.

Marriage Preparation and Tools

Marriage preparation is an essential enterprise for the church to accompany her faithful to embrace the mystery that sacramental marriage represents. The cultural shift today impacts society and the Church as well. This makes it necessary to get engaged couples to consider the complexities that diversity brings and the issues that confront the institution of marriage. Pope Francis, in *Amoris Laetitia,* puts it in clear terms when he says, "The complexity of today's society and the challenges faced by the family require a greater effort on the part of the whole Christian community in preparing those who are about to be married."[131] Some young people no longer see sacramental marriage as a witness but instead as a means of self-satisfaction and development and hence do not see success as dependent on the community's support. They now see their success merging from within, and there is a need to restore sacramental marriage as a public affair expressing its revelatory reality. The process must consider the involvement of the faith community to "recognize the great benefit they receive from supporting engaged couples as they grow in love."[132] Pope Francis continues that "marriage preparation should be a kind of "initiation" to the sacrament of matrimony, providing couples with the help they need to receive the sacrament worthily and to make a solid beginning of life as a family."[133] The process that can meet the needs of young people today must be extensive and sensitive to issues that confront society. The process must help engaged couples grow in love and mature in their readiness to commit to what the sacrament demands.

The *National Directory for Catechesis* states that *"catechesis for the sacrament of Matrimony is addressed to the* parish community. It is addressed directly to couples intending to marry in the parish and often takes the form of a diocesan or parish preparation program.[134]" Any preparation model being adopted must bear in mind that engaged couples marry in a community of faith and for witness within that community. This is why it is essential to pay attention to the faith journey of each couple and help them connect how their union ought to be a witness of God's relationship with His Church. The *Directory* recommends that each diocese must adopt resources that "encourage the care and concern of the whole Christian community for married couples by public recognition of couples planning a marriage, modeling by couples in successful marriages, and support of couples in challenged marriages, and stresses marriage as a distinct and dignified vocation in the Church."[135]

I believe that it is more fruitful when marriage preparation takes into consideration the individual situations of couples. Engaging the couples to determine how many sessions are needed is essential because only some couples have the exact needs. Marriage preparation should allow the engaged couple to discuss issues they may not have considered while dating. This is where the inventories become helpful in providing insights, and the sessions offer platforms to have intentional discussions on issues that might arise. One weekend event may not be ideal or enough to connect what the Church is asking of them and the issues that need to be discussed. During these sessions, engaged couples can elaborate discussions on issues like children, finances, family backgrounds, cultural biases, and conflict resolution. On another note, marriage between a catholic and someone who practices another faith takes even more process or instruction because the engaged couple needs to explore each other's faith more carefully, as well as understand the obligations the non-Catholic person has in this marriage.

Diana Macalintal and Nick Wagner discuss four indispensable tools that must not be overlooked in any marriage preparation. According to them, the tools are "word, community, worship, and witness.[136] The engaged couples need to see their journey through the scripture. The scripture is the foundation of the sacrament they are about to undertake. They begin to unpack their experience of God's revelation in the scripture, growing in their relationship with Christ. This is the beauty of the catechumenate model when we do not approach the preparation process with the mindset of the classroom but allow a dynamic journey of faith through the word of God and Church teachings. When engaged couples grow in the love of Christ through catechesis, it is easier for them to connect what they pray and believe in their daily lives. The second tool mentioned by Diana and Nick is the community, this already exists with the parish family, but the process must find a way to involve the members in the preparation. There are indirect and direct ways to involve the parish members in this way; we draw the engaged couples deeper into the parish life. An instance of ways to involve the community like the one suggested in the book, *Joined by Church, sealed by a Blessing*, "Wedding Welcoming Ministry."[137] There are activities already happening in the parish; the process needs to find a way to connect the engaged couples to get involved in parish life. Worship as a tool entails creating the opportunity for the members to actively participate in the liturgy, which is the center of parish life. The last tool, the witness, must help the couple appreciate the sacrament of marriage as a revelatory reality, and they need to experience that reality with the parish members. At the same time, they prepare to enter it.

According to Diana and Nick, "Our couples already come to us with hearts on fire with love for each other and a desire to celebrate that love in the rituals of the Church. Your call as ministers responsible for their vocational preparation is to give them all the tools, they need to keep that fire burning."[138] The resources must reflect these needs and incorporate these four tools; the catechumenate model provides the platform and creates the opportunity for a conscious engagement of the couples and the parish community to journey with them.

There are resources and tools available to dioceses and parishes that engage couples to deepen their faith in God and understand the sacrament intentionally. Each diocese or parish is unique, and the resources to be used must consider the needs of the people. Some inventories are available such as FOCCUS, Prepare-Enrich, and FACET. Some weekend retreat events for engaged couples, like Pre-Cana and Unveiled, are used by the Diocese of Richmond. There is another retreat option called Engaged Encounter, which allows the couples to focus on their commitment to each other and the implications of their commitment as they prepare to enter fully into the sacrament. However good these opportunities are, there should be one-on-one sessions between the engaged couples and the priest, the deacon, or the team. It should be noted that the inventories are lovely, but the facilitators need to be equipped with the essential skills necessary for fruitful results.

Dian and Nick are correct when they remarked that "no amount of reading, listening, or talking can teach us (engaged couples) fully how to be married once the wedding is over."[139] Those intending to marry in the church need to be engaged and allowed to connect the lessons with real-life situations directly or indirectly. The process must be such that it "helps couples to practice the skills and attitudes of married life. They learn to forgive not simply by reading about forgiveness or talking about it, not even understanding that they should forgive. They learn to forgive and become forgiving people by forgiving. They learn to sacrifice themselves to one another by sacrificing themselves in big and small ways to others daily."[140] One resource that I find good is *Witness to Love*. The structure provides an opportunity to engage the couples with other 'successful' married couples and help them deepen their commitment and understanding of the sacrament.

Ryan and Mary-Rose Verret have beautiful insights from their encounter with couples and engaged couples that taught them that "the insights of close, loving young couples and family provide a valuable reality check to young couples."[141] *Witness to Love* contains vital ingredients for a fruitful marriage preparation incorporating the catechumenate model that treats the sacrament as a witness and a community affair.

With the catechumenate model and in the context of the *Witness to Love* resource, the sessions for marriage preparation will last between eight to ten sessions, and an intentional effort to connect them to small groups after the wedding. I will have to prepare the team with the skill to use the inventory tool; prepare Enrich as my favorite because of its dynamics. I will also encourage the team to be spontaneous and not rigid in their presentations and working with the couples and will discover each person's strengths. My first meeting will be focused on building rapport with the engaged couples and getting to know them and their backgrounds, followed by the pre-nuptial forms and discussions on how the process will go. In this first meeting, I will explain the parish's vision, how the sessions will go, and their expectations. I find how the Archdiocese of Portland structures its sessions. They have eight steps process, which is as follows: initial meeting: Forms and Inventory invite, coaching session and Inventory Review, Sponsor and Engage Couple meeting, Retreat, Theology Discussion, Parish Welcome and Connect to Small Groups, Review and Wedding Day, Continued Parish Accompaniment (Post Wedding).[142] It is necessary to invest in the team to help them understand their role in the process. Another aspect is to pay attention to how the cultural shift and expressive individualism have impacted how sacramental marriage is embraced, which means that "this mentor-less generation desperately needs witnesses of sacrificial and enduring marital love."[143]

Each of the eight sessions must consider how the couples respond to materials. It is essential to respect the couples' privacy; it is good to have the inventory review with the mentors present if the couples are comfortable with that. Having the coaching session and inventory review together allows the mentors to witness the engaged couples. The theology discussion can happen in any other sessions if need be, but leaving the theology discussion after the retreat is to give the couples a chance to share their concerns and have an intentional discussion on what the Church intends. God's plan is for married couples. *Witness to Love* provides questions on key themes to engage the couples to share and be open to insights. The questions center on communication skills, finance, relationship with God, managing and resolving conflicts, sex, sexuality, etc.

Chapter 7
Marriage Mentor Program Proposal

This initiative aims to enrich our practical marriage preparation through mentor relationships, expanded resources, and an intentional plan of engagement that begins at marriage preparation and accompanies couples through the first few years of marriage. The Mentor Couples would focus on practical marriage formation, while the clergy would continue the sacramental formation aspects. In addition to the enriching formation before the wedding, this program would extend pastoral care, support, and opportunities for evangelization after the wedding day and when many couples begin families and seek formation for Baptism.

Mentor Couples Characteristics to Consider

- Mentor Couples be married for at least ten years.
    - There may be valuable roles for couples married less than ten years to play.

- Both spouses are Catholic.
  - Similar ministries suggested there may be value in having mixed-faith couples minister to the increasing number of mixed-faith couples getting married.
- Stable, healthy, faithful couples
  - Similar ministries indicated that a few of their mentor couples ended up getting divorced. We should consider how to address the health of a Mentor Couple's relationship and how to assist them when needed.
  - Mentor Couples should recognize that fidelity to church teaching is imperative.

Mentor Couples Discernment Phase

- **Nomination**
  - Prospective Mentor Couples will be identified primarily through Pastor and Staff Recommendations.
- **Retreat**
  - Couples will be invited to attend a retreat to reflect on their journey, enrich their marriage, and discern their involvement as a Mentor Couple in this ministry.

- **Review**
  - Clergy and lay marriage formation ministers could meet with couples through an interview/meeting process.

Formation of Mentor Couples

- Mentor Couples would be trained using the Prepare/Enrich resources/materials.
- Mentor Couples should understand the stages of evangelization to identify and respond to the needs of couples in phases of pre-evangelization or various levels of engagement.

Ministry Structure

- **What we know**
  - Mentor and Mentee couples should meet with some frequency before marriage and some frequency after marriage.
  - Quarterly Enrichment workshops will be offered on various topics and, as appropriate, will be available to both engaged and newly married couples. (See proposed workshop details below)
  - Mentor and Mentee couples will be grouped based on shared interests/common ground.

- **Details to figure out.**
  - Do Mentor Couples take over some aspects of what clergy currently offer, especially assessments?
  - With what frequency do we contact couples in marriage prep/post-marriage?
  - Does a couple get new mentors after Marriage?
  - Do mentors assess the mentee's level of engagement? What are those metrics, and how do we respond to each metric?
    - One idea is to use unaffiliated, marginally active, and very active as metrics, with specific contacts based on each level of engagement.
  - A list of topics and presenters for workshops.

Proposed responses to couples according to the level of engagement

- **1st Level of Engagement: Unaffiliated**
  - Phone calls/text/social media check-ins every few months.
  - Asking if they need help (networking, social, moving, finances, marriage, child raising, etc.)
  - Sharing upcoming events
  - Invitations to dinner/gatherings

- **2nd Level of Engagement: Moderately affiliated**
  - All of level 1

- Reaching out when they aren't seen for a week or two at Masses.
- Invitations to social, catechetical events, low commitment ministries
- Invitations to Dinners and Workshops

- **3rd Level of Engagement**
  - All of Levels 1 and 2
  - Invitations to active ministry
  - Invitation to be Newly Wed Contributors to assist other couples in formation as a voice of the newly married.

Conclusion

Culture and marriage are two concepts that are deeply intertwined in human societies. Culture shapes the norms, values, expectations, and practices of marriage, while marriage influences the transmission, adaptation, and evolution of culture. In this book, we explore the fascinating diversity and complexity of culture and marriage across the world, from ancient times to the present day.

We examine how different cultures define, celebrate, regulate, and challenge marriage, and how marriage affects the identity, status, rights, and obligations of individuals and groups. We also analyze how culture and marriage interact with other social institutions, such as religion, politics, economy, education, and health. We highlight the commonalities and differences among various forms of marriage, such as monogamy, polygamy, arranged, love, same-sex, and intercultural marriages, and the implications of these forms for the well-being of individuals, families, and societies.

This book is intended for anyone interested in learning more about the rich and diverse aspects of culture and marriage, friendship, and the dynamic relationship between them. We hope that this book will inspire readers to reflect on their own cultural and marital experiences and to appreciate the diversity and complexity of human cultures and marriages. This book is ideal for those considering marriage, those who are married, and those who prepare couples, and for churches to find necessary tools to support couples in their marriage.

Footnotes

[1] Catechism of the Catholic Church, #2364.

[2] Fulton Sheen. *Three to Get Married,* (New York: Scepter Publishers, Inc., 1951), p. 34.

[3] Michael G. Lawler. *Marriage and the Catholic Church: Disputed Questions.* Minnesota: The Liturgical Press, 2002. p. 98.

[4] Beal, Coriden, and Green, p. 1259.

[5] Lawler. p. 99.

[6] Lawler. p. 99.

[7] Mackin, S.J., p. 210.

[8] Lawler. p. 100.

[9] Schillebeeckx, p. 31.

[10] Schillebeeckx., p. 32.

[11] Schillebeeckx, p. 38.

[12] Schillebeeckx, P. 116.

[13] Schillebeeckx, P. 116.

[14] Schillebeeckx, p. 116.

[15] United Bishops Conference. *Marriage: Love and Life in the Divine Plan,* (Washington, D.C, 2009), p. 43.

[16] Francis Nemeck and Marie Coombs. *Discerning Vocations to Marriage, Celibacy and Singlehood,* (Oregon: Wipf and Stock Publishers, 2001),p. 43.

[17] Javier Abad and Eugenio Fenoy. *Marriage: A Path to Sanctity,* (Manila: Sinag-Tala Publishers, INC. 2002), p. 34.

[18] Nemeck and Coombs. p. 44.

[19] Unites States Catholic Bishops, p. 44.

[20] Regis and Libbie Flaherty. *The Sacrament of Marriage as Vocation,* (Steubenville: Emmaus Road Publishing, 2007), p. 7.

[21] Daniel Zopoula. *The All-for-Nothing Marriage,* (Canada: Friesen Press, 2019) p. 31.

[22] Frantz Mars. *Seeking Love, marriage, and Family,* (United States: Xlibris Press, 2014), p 154.

[23] Reynolds, p. 2.

[24] Ouellet, p. 17.

[25] United States Catholic Bishops Conference, p. 32.

[26] United States Catholic Bishops Conference, p. 32.

[27] Lawler, p. 54.

[28] United States Catholic Bishops Conference, p. 33..

[29] United States Catholic Bishops Conference, pp. 33-34.

[30] *National Directory for Catechesis.* (Washington, D.C: United States Conference of Catholic Bishops, 2005), 29.

[31] Cherlin, p. 157.

[32] Edward Wimberly, C*ounseling African American Marriages and Families.* (Kentucky: Westminster John Knox Press, 1997), p.1.

[33] Cherlin, p. 134.

³⁴ Catholic Church and Francis, Encyclical Letter *Amoris Laetitia.* (United States: Bacon Publishing, 2015), par. 294.

³⁵ Stephen Grunlan, Marvin Mayers. *Cultural Anthropology: A Christian Perspective,* (Grand Rapids: Zondervan, 2016), P. 54.

³⁶ Grunlan, Meyers, p. 55.

³⁷ LeNora Millen. *The Power of Self-Reclaiming the "I am,"* (*India:* Author House, 2012), pp. 80-81.

³⁸ Mariasusai Dhavmony. *Christian Theology of Inculturation.,* (*Rome*: Editrice Pontifica Universita Gregoriana, 1997), P. 27.

³⁹ Dhavmony, p. 28.

⁴⁰ George Maduakolam Okorie. *The Integral Salvation of the Human Person in Ecclesia in Africa: A Case Study of the Theological Implications among the Igbo in Nigeria.* (Frankfurt: Peter Lang GmbH, 2007), P. 182.

⁴¹ Okorie, p. 184.

⁴² Okorie, p. 186.

⁴³ Okorie, p. 186.

⁴⁴ Okorie, p. 187.

⁴⁵ Okorie, p. 190.

⁴⁶ Cherlin, p. 24.

⁴⁷ Cherlin, p. 26.

⁴⁸ Cherlin, p. 30.

⁴⁹ *The Rites, Vol. 1.* (New York: Pueblo Publishing Company, no.3, 1990),720.

[50]. Plato, *Lysis.* trans by Harold North Fowler (Cambridge, MA: Harvard University Press, 1975),43.

[51] John Scudder and Anne Bishop. *Beyond Friendship and Eros: Unrecognized Relationships between Men and Women.* (Albany, New York: States University of New York Press, 2001), p. 60.

[52] David Bolotin. *Plato's Dialogue on Friendship: An interpretation of the 'Lysis",* with a New Translation. (Ithaca: Cornell University Press, 1989), p. 67.

[53] Josephine M. Ford, *Redeemer: Friend and Mother: Salvation in Antiquity and in the Gospel of John* (Minneapolis: Fortress Press, 1997), p. 79.

[54] Gabriel R. Lear: *Happy Lives and the Highest Good: An Essay on Aristotle's Nichomachean Ethics* (Princeton University Press, 2009), p. 29.

[55] Lorraine Smith Pangle. *Aristotle and the Philosophy of Friendship.* (New York: Cambridge University Press, 2008), p. 7.

[56] Aristotle, *Nicomachean Ethics,* trans. Terrence Irwin (Indianapolis: Hackett, 1999), BK IX #30 Par. 3, p. 152.

[57] Marcus Tullius Cicero, translated by Philip Freeman. *How to be a friend: an ancient guide to true friendship.* (Princeton: Princeton University press, 2018), xi-xii.

[58] Marcus Tullius Cicero, translated by E.S. Shuckburgh. *Treatise on Friendship and Old Age* (Westland, MI: Brian Westland Publishing company, 2019), p. 18. (Come back to this)

[59] Marcus Tullius Cicero, (come back to this) translated by E.S. Shuckburgh. *Treatise on Friendship and Old Age* (Brian Westland Publishing company, 2019), p. 21.

⁶⁰ Marcia L. Colish *The Stoic Tradition from Antiquity to the Early Middle Ages: II. Stoicism in Christian Latin Thought Through the Sixth Century* (Leiden, Netherlands: Brill, 1985), p. 41.

⁶¹ Augustine confessions, Trans R.S. Pine-Coffin (London: Penguin Books, 1978), Bk II.5. p. 10.

⁶² For Augustine, the bond of marriage is the foundation for friendship and affective union of the spouses. He further specified its growth in charity, the sanctifying gift of the Holy Spirit. (see Paul Rigby, *The Theology of Augustine's Confessions,* New York: Cambridge University Press, 2015), p. 225.

⁶³ Donald X. Burt. *Friendship and Society: An Introduction to Augustine's Practical Philosophy.* (Grand Rapids, Mich: W.B. Eerdmans, 1999), p. 8.

⁶⁴ Kim Paffenroth. "Friendship as Personal, Social, and Theological Virtue in Augustine." In *Augustine and Politics.* John Doody, Kevin L. Hughes, and Kim Paffenroth editors (Lanham, MD: Lexington Books, 2010), p. 63.

⁶⁵ Augustine's Confessions trans R.S. Pine-Coffin, Bk IV.4. p. 7.

⁶⁶ Paul Helm. Augustine's Griefs in *Confessions*: Critical Essays, ed. by William E. Mann. (Lanham, MD: Rowman & Littlefield, 2006), p. 147.

⁶⁷ Augustine. Trans Robin Lane Fox *Conversions to Confessions.* (New York: Basic Books, 2017), p. 58.

⁶⁸ Augustine's Confessions, Bk IV.14. p. 24.

⁶⁹ Paul J. Waddell. *Becoming Friends: Worship, Justice, and the Practice of Christian Friendship* (Quezon City, Philippines, 2004), p. 83-84

[70] Waddell, *Becoming Friends*, p. 85.

[71] Waddell, *Becoming Friends*, p. 86.

[72] Augustine, *De Bono Conuigali, 3* in Edward Ferdinand Rogers, *Theology and Sexuality: Classic and Contemporary Readings.* (Malden, MA: Blackwell Publishing, 2017), p. 123.

[73] In De Bono Conjugali, 9, Augustine describes marriage as an instrumental good: surely it must be acknowledged that God gave us some goods to be sought for their own sake, such as wisdom, good health, and friendship, and others that are necessary for the sake of something else, such as learning, food, drink, sleep, marriage are sexual intercourse. Some are necessary for good health, such as food and drink and sleep; and some are necessary for friendship, such as marriage and sexual intercourse, for these lead to the propagation of the human race, in which a friendly association is a great good.

[74] Thomas Aquinas, *Summa Theologiae,* 2nd, rev. ed., trans. Fathers of the English Dominican Province (1920; New Advent, 2008): II-II p. .23. (check this further)

[75] James C. Goig, *Aquinas' Philosophical Commentary on the 'ethics': A Historical Perspective.* (Dordrecht, Netherlands: Kluwer Academic Publishers, 2001), p. 72.

[76] James Conroy Doig, *Aquinas's Philosophical Commentary on the Ethics: A Historical Perspective.* Dordrecht: Springer,2015), p. 71.

[77] Thomas Aquinas, *Summa Theologiae,* II-II. p. 60.1.

[78] Bernard V. Brady, *Christian Love* (Washington, D.C: Georgetown University Press, 2015), p. 167

[79] Dominic Legge, *The Trinitarian Christology of St. Thomas Aquinas* (New York: Oxford University Press, 2018), p. 13.

[80] Matthew Kauth, *Charity As Divine and Human Friendship: A Metaphysical and Scriptural Explanation According to the Thought of St. Thomas Aquinas.* (Rome: Saint Benedict Press, 2012), p. 121.

[81] John 15:15

[82] Waddle, *Becoming Friends,* p. 64.

[83] Aquinas, *Summa Theologiae,* I-II. p. 65.5.

[84] Fulton J. Sheen, *Three to Get Married,* (Princeton, NJ: Scepter Publishers, 1951), p. 188.

[85] Donald X. Burt, *Friendship and Society: An Introduction to Augustine's Practical Philosophy* (Grand Rapids, MI.: W.B. Eerdmans Publ. 1999), p. 87.

[86] Aquinas, *Summa Contra Gentiles*, trans. Vernon J. Bourke. (London: University of Notre Dame Press, 1975), III.p. 126.

[87] Thomas Aquinas, *Summa Contra Gentiles*.3. p. 124.

[88] Aristotle, *Nicomachean Ethics,* BK VIII, 2.

[89] Aquinas, *Summa Contra Gentiles*, III. p. 123. 6.

[90] Aquinas, *Summa Theologiae,* I-II. p. 142. 1

[91] Aquinas, *Summa Theologiae,* III. p. 29 .2.

[92] Aquinas, *Summa Theologiae,* III. p. 29. 2.

[93] Aquinas, *Summa Theologiae,* I-III. p. 28. 3.

[94] Brady, *Christian Love, p.* 169.

[95] Aquinas, *Summa Theologiae*, III, p. 29.2.

[96] USCCB, *Marriage: Love and life in the Divine Plan.* (Washington, D.C.: United States Conference of Catholic Bishops, 2010), p. 10.

[97] Gordon P. Hugenberger. *Marriage as a Covenant: Biblical Law and Ethics as developed from Malachi.* (Eugene, Oregon: WIPF and Stock Publishers, 2014), p. 11.

[98] Michael Lawler. *Marriage and Sacrament: A Theology of Christian Marriage.* (Collegeville, Minn: Liturgical Press, 1993), p. 12.

[99] Marriage "must include a liturgical celebration before a priest, two witnesses and the assembly of the church. See, Gregory L. Klein and Robert A. Wolfe, *Pastoral Foundations of the Sacraments: A Catholic Perspective.* (New York: Paulist Press, 1998), p. 136.

[100] Klein and Wolfe. *Pastoral Foundations of the Sacrament,* p. 136.

[101] Pope Benedict XVI Ominium in Mentem http://www.vatican.va/content/benedict-xvi/en/apost_letters/documents/hf_ben-xvi_apl_20091026_codex-iuris-canonici.html accessed August 6, 2020.Para. 5

[102] *Pontifical Council for The Family,* p. 35.

[103] *Familiaris Consortio, no.*13.

[104] Cahall, *The Mystery of Marriage, p.* 78-79.

[105] Harold Burke-Sivers, *Behold the Man: A Catholic Vision of Male Spirituality* (San Francisco, CA: Ignatius Press, 2015), p. 132.

[106] *Familiaris Consortio,* 13.

107 Edward Schillebeeckx. *Marriage: Human Reality and Saving Mystery.* (London: Sheed and Ward,1988), p. 326.

108 Pope Benedict XVI, Encyclical Letter, *Deus Caritas Est* [On Christian Love] (http://www.vatican.va/content/benedict-xvi/en/encyclicals/documents/hf_ben-xvi_enc_20051225_deus-caritas-est.html accessed May 17, 2020, p 25.

109 Herbert Vorgrimler. *Sacramental Theology.* (Collegeville, Minn: Liturgical Press, 1992), p 25.

110 Pope Benedict XVI Solemnity of Corpus Christi http://w2.vatican.va/content/benedict-xvi/en/homilies/2011/documents/hf_ben-xvi_hom_20110623_corpus-domini.html accessed August 7, 2020, para. 4.

111 USCCB. *United States Catholic Catechism for Adults* (Cincinnati, OH: St. Anthony Messenger Press, 2006), p 283.

112 USCCB, *Marriage: Love and Life in the Divine Plan.* (Washington, D.C.: United States conference of Catholic Bishops, 2010), p. 53.

113 Pontifical Council for the Family, p. 16.

114 Familiaris Consortio, p. 51.

115 God's love is sacramentally communicated in every human encounter, whether it be interpersonal, group, or inter-group, and people are called to respond to that love through these relationships. see Brian Hearne. *Theology: Basic Course* (Eldoret: AMECEA Pastoral Institute, 1976), p 30.

[116] USCCB, *United States Catholic Catechism for Adults*. (Cincinnati, OH: St. Anthony Messenger Press, 2006), p 281.

[117] Benezeri Kisembo, Magesa Laurenti, and Aylward Shorter. *African Christian Marriage*. (Nairobi: Paulines Publications Africa, 2015), p 41.

[118] Vorgrimler, *Sacramental Theology*, p. 27.

[119] Lawler, *Marriage and Sacrament*, 14.

[120] USCCB, *National directory for Catechesis* (Washington, D.C.: United States Conference of catholic Bishops, 2005), p 97-98.

[121] Donald X. Burt. *Friendship and Society: An Introduction to Augustine's Practical Philosophy*. (Grand Rapids, Mich: W.B. Eerdmans, 1999), *p.* 83.

[122] Aquinas, *Summa Theologiae* III. p. 29. 2

[123] Kisembo, Magesa, and Shorter, *African Christian Marriage,* p 42.

[124] The United States Conference of Catholic Bishops. *National Directory for Catechesis*. (Washington, D.C.: United States Conference of Catholic Bishops, 2005), p 115.

[125] The United States Conference of Catholic Bishops, p. 116.

[126] Fintan Gavin, *Pastoral Care in marriage Preparation (Can. 1063): History, Analysis of the Norm and its Implementation by Some Particular Churches*. (Roma: Pontificia University Gregoriana, 2004), p 67.

[127] Fintan, p.67

[128] Fintan, p. 67-68.

[129] Catholic Church and Francis, Encyclical Letter. *Amoris Laetitia.* (United States: Beacon Publishing, 2015), par. 293.

[130] Catholic Church and John Paul 11. Encyclical Letter, *Familiaris Consortio.* (Washington D.C.: United States Conference, 1982), Par. 66.

[131] Catholic Church and Francis. Encyclical Letter, *Amoris Laetitia.* (United States: Beacon Publishing, 2015), par. 206.

[132] Catholic Church and Francis. Encyclical Letter, *Amoris Laetitia.* (United States: Beacon Publishing, 2015), par.207.

[133] Catholic Church and Francis. Encyclical Letter, *Amoris Laetitia.* (United States: Beacon Publishing, 2015), par. 207.

[134] United States Conference of Catholic Bishops, p. 142.

[135] United States Conference of Catholic Bishops., p. 143.

[136] Diana Macalintal and Nick Wagner, joined *by the Church, Sealed by a Blessing,* (Minnesota: Liturgical Press, 2014), p.39.

[137] Diana Macalintal and Nick Wagner, joined *by the Church, Sealed by a Blessing,* (Minnesota: Liturgical Press, 2014), p.39.[137] Macalintal and Wagner, p. 47.

[138] Macalintal and Wagner, p. 68.

[139] Macalintal and Wagner, p. 34.

[140] Macalintal and Wagner, p .34.

[141] Verret, Ryan and Mary-Rose. *Witness to Love.* (North Carolina: St. Benedict Press, 2015), p. 2.

[142] Archdiocese of Portland, Oregon. *Marriage and Family Office. https://famlife.archdpdx.org/parish-marriage-prep* accessed on 12/3/2018.

[143] Verret, p.51.

References

Aquinas, Thomas. *Summa Theologiae:* Complete English Edition in Five Volumes. Trans. Fathers of the English Dominican Province. Westminster, MD: Christian Classic, 2008.

Aristotle. *Nicomachean Ethics* BK III Trans. Terrence Irwin Indianapolis: Hackett, 1999.

Augustine. *Confessions*, Trans R.S. Pine-Coffin London: Penguin Books, 1978.

Augustine. *Conversions to Confessions.* Translated by Robin, Fox. New York: Basic Books, 2017.

Augustine. *De Bono Conuigali,* Volume 3. Translated by Edward, F. Rogers. In Theology and Sexuality: Classic and Contemporary Readings. Hoboken, NJ: Blackwell Publishing, 2017.

Augustine. *The Confessions of St. Augustine*: Books I-X. Trans. F. J. Sheed. Kansas City: Sheed Andrews and McMeel, 1970.

Benedict XVI, Pope. Apostolic Letter, *Ominium in Mentem* [On Several Amendments to the Code of Canon Law] http://www.vatican.va/content/benedict xvi/en/apost_letters/documents/hf_ben-xvi_apl_20091026_codex-iuris-canonici.html accessed August 6, 2020.

Benedict XVI, Pope. Encyclical Letter, *Deus Caritas Est* [On Christian Love] (http://www.vatican.va/content/benedict-xvi/en/encyclicals/documents/hf_ben xvi_enc_20051225_deus-caritas-est.html accessed May 17, 2020.

Benedict XVI, Pope. Homily, *Solemnity of Corpus Christi.* http://w2.vatican.va/content/benedict xvi/en/homilies/2011/documents/hf_ben-xvi_hom_20110623_corpus-domini.htmlaccessed August 7, 2020.

Brady, Bernard V. *Christian Love.* Washington, D.C: Georgetown University Press, 2015.

Burt, Donald X. *Friendship and Society: An Introduction to Augustine's Practical Philosophy.* Grand Rapids, Mich: W.B. Eerdmans, 1999.

Catholic Bishops, 2005.

Cicero, Marcus Tullius. *How to be a Friend: An Ancient Guide to True Friendship.* Trans. by Philip Freeman. Princeton: Princeton University Press, 2018.

Cicero, Marcus Tullius. Treatise on Friendship and Old Age. Trans. Shuckburg, E.S. London Westland Publishing company, 2019.

Colish, Marcia L. *The Stoic Tradition from Antiquity to the Early Middle Ages: II. Stoicism in Christian Latin Thought Through the Sixth Century.* Leiden, Netherlands: Brill, 1985.

Doig, James Conroy. *Aquinas's Philosophical Commentary on the Ethics: A Historical Perspective.* Dordrecht, Netherlands: Springer, 2015.

Ford, Josephine M. *Redeemer: Friend and Mother: Salvation in Antiquity and in the Gospel of John.* Minneapolis: Fortress Press, 1997.

Helm, Paul. *Augustine's Griefs in Augustine's Confessions: Critical Essays* ed by William E. Mann. Lanham, MD: Rowman & Littlefield, 2006.

Hugenberger, Gordon P. *Marriage as a Covenant: Biblical Law and Ethics as developed from Malachi.* Eugene, Oregon: WIPF and Stock Publishers, 2014.

John Paul II, Pope. Apostolic Exhortation, *Familiaris Consortio* [The Role of the Christian Family in the Modern World]. Boston: Pauline Books and Media, 2015.

Kauth, Matthew. *Charity As Divine and Human Friendship: A Metaphysical and Scriptural Explanation According to the Thought of St. Thomas Aquinas.* Rome: Saint Benedict Press, 2012.

Kisembo, Benezeri, Laurenti Magesa, and Aylward Shorter. *African Christian Marriage.* Nairobi: Pauline Publications Africa, 2015.

Klein, Gregory L. and Wolfe, Robert A. *Pastoral Foundations of the Sacraments: A Catholic Perspective.* New York: Paulist Press, 1998.

Lawler, Michael. *Marriage and Sacrament: A Theology of Christian Marriage.* Collegeville, MI: Liturgical Press, 1993.

Legge, Dominic. *The Trinitarian Christology of St. Thomas Aquinas.* New York: Oxford University Press, 2018.

Paffenroth, Kim. "Friendship as Personal, Social, and Theological Virtue in Augustine". In *Augustine and Politics.* Edited by John Doody, Kevin L. Hughes, and Kim Paffenroth. Lanham, MD: Lexington Books, 2010.

Pangle, Lorraine S. *Aristotle and the Philosophy of Friendship.* New York: Cambridge University Press, 2008.

Plato, *Lysis.* Trans. Harold North Fowler. Cambridge, Mass: Harvard University Press, 1975.

Schillebeeckx, Edward. *Marriage: Human Reality and Saving Mystery.* London: Sheed and Ward, 1988.

Scudder, John & Bishop, Anne. *Beyond Friendship and Eros: Unrecognized Relationships between Men and Women.* Albany, New York: States University of New York Press, 2001.

Sheen, Fulton J. *Three to Get Married*. Princeton, New Jersey: Scepter Publishers, 2004.

USCCB. *Marriage: Love and Life in the Divine Plan*. Washington, D.C, 2009.

---. *National Directory for Catechesis*. Washington, D.C: United States Conference of

---. *The Rites of the Catholic Church*. Vol. 1. New York: Pueblo Publishing Company, 1990.

Vatican Council II, *Gaudium et Spes* [Pastoral Constitution on the Church in the Modern World In Vatican Council II: The Conciliar and Post Conciliar Documents Vol. 1. Edited by. Austin Flannery, O.P., 910-911. 5th ed. Rev. ed. Northport, NY: Costello Publishing Company, 2004.

Vorgrimler, Herbert. *Sacramental Theology*. Collegeville, Minn: Liturgical Press, 1992.

Waddell, Paul J. *Becoming Friends: Worship, Justice, and the Practice of Christian Friendship*. Quezon City, Philippines, Claretian Publications, 2004.

Lear, Gabriel Richardson. Happy Lives and the Highest Good: An Essay on Aristotle's Nicomachean Ethics. New Jersey: Princeton University Press, 2009.

Rev. Tochi Iwuji

Rev. Tochi Iwuji is a Catholic Priest, Pastor, and Pastoral Counselor with a specialty in Marriage and Family. Rev. Iwuji has graduate degrees in pastoral Counseling, a Master of Divinity, a Master of Theology, and a Licentiate of Sacred Theology (Moral Theology). Rev. Iwuji is a spiritual director, keynote speaker, and consultant. He can be reached at www.FatherTochi.org.

NOTES

NOTES

NOTES

NOTES

NOTES

www.ingramcontent.com/pod-product-compliance
Lightning Source LLC
Chambersburg PA
CBHW051622010526
44119CB00039B/477/J